PUFFIN BOOKS

TAATUNG TATUNG AND OTHER AMAZING STORIES OF INDIA'S DIVERSE LANGUAGES

Vaishali Shroff is an award-winning author, script writer, and columnist based in Mumbai. She has published over 200 stories in books and other media across Indian and international publishing houses. She loves writing about unexplored places, untold histories, and unheard voices.

Some of her works include *The Adventures of Padma and a Blue Dinosaur*, winner of the 2019 Best in Indian Children's Writing (BICW) award, *Sita's Chitwan*, listed as one of the Top 10 Noteworthy Books of 2021 by *Times of India*, *There's a Leopard in My House*, winner of the ECA-APER award for Best Fiction Book for Children, and *Batata, Pao and All Things Portuguese*, winner of New Voices in Non-fiction Scholarship offered by SCBWI, US. Her debut short movie as a script writer, *Rajasaur*, has been screened and has won multiple awards for Best Short Film across film festivals in the US and India.

Shroff loves talking to children over adults, chocolate over anything else, and wants to be a tree in her next life. Follow her @vaishaliwrites on Instagram to know more about her work.

ADVANCE PRAISE FOR THE BOOK

'In *Taatung Tatung*, Vaishali Shroff covers the full spectrum of India's glorious linguistic tradition, from the well-known (the trials of the Bangla Language Movement) to the fascinating and overlooked (the powerful symbolism of Hijra Farsi). This book is an eye-opening examination of a critical aspect of our culture, as well as a warning against allowing languages and their rich legacies to disappear'—Dr Shashi Tharoor, Member of the Lok Sabha

'This well-researched and easy-to-read book brings home to readers the tremendous language diversity of India. The delightful narratives in it form for the young readers a fascinating introduction to India's linguistic riches. A much, much needed work'—Ganesh N. Devy, Chair, People's Linguistic Survey of India

'Amazing and enjoyable . . . this is a book on the survival and sustenance of languages forewarning us as to what happens when languages vanish from the face of the earth robbing us of a significant piece in the puzzle of language evolution. The lucid and friendly style that Vaishali Shroff employs will be immensely cherished by children and adults alike'—Anvita Abbi, Padma Shri, Linguist

'A brilliant people's history of the subcontinent using interesting stories of the various intertwined languages spoken here over the centuries . . . A must read'—Shubhranshu Choudhary, Journalist and Peace Activist

'A must-read for everyone to understand the role of language beyond everyday communication. A call for action to preserve our cultural identities'—Kalika Bali, Computational Linguist, Microsoft Research

TAATUNG TATUNG

AND OTHER AMAZING STORIES OF INDIA'S DIVERSE LANGUAGES

VAISHALI SHROFF

ILLUSTRATIONS BY
ADRIJA GHOSH

PUFFIN BOOKS
An imprint of Penguin Random House

PUFFIN BOOKS

USA | Canada | UK | Ireland | Australia
New Zealand | India | South Africa | China

Puffin Books is part of the Penguin Random House group of companies
whose addresses can be found at global.penguinrandomhouse.com

Published by Penguin Random House India Pvt. Ltd
4th Floor, Capital Tower 1, MG Road,
Gurugram 122 002, Haryana, India

| Penguin
Random House
India

First published in Puffin Books by Penguin Random House India 2023

Text copyright © Vaishali Shroff 2023
Illustration copyright © Adrija Ghosh 2023

ISBN 9780143454663

Book design and layout by Isha Nagar
Typeset in EB Garamond by Manipal Technologies Limited, Manipal
Printed at Replika Press Pvt. Ltd, India

www.penguin.co.in

For Arinjay and Vivikt

CONTENTS

Contents

Death of Languages

Revitalization and Rebirth of Languages

INTRODUCTION

The swaying of trees tells us there's a breeze. The dark clouds in the sky tell us it may rain. The blooming tulips tell us it's spring, while the laburnum trees with clusters of sunshine hanging from their branches tell us that summer is here. Everything around us communicates—creatures as small as ants use body language to communicate with each other, the bees do the waggle dance, and the mighty whales have their own songs!

Everything around us has a language.

Call it *glossa* in Greek, *tungumal* in Icelandic, *lingua* in Latin, *language* in English or *bhasha* in Hindi. Call a language anything in the thousands of different languages in the world. Yet, try to remove it from our world, and we will be left with no world at all.

No matter what linguists have proved or tried to prove over centuries, no one has been able to accurately explain how languages came into existence. It's practically impossible to trace the origin of communication of languages. This is why how languages came into existence and how they evolved is always debatable.

Languages are living entities. They evolve over time—they are born, they grow, they adapt, they change, and they even die. It's said that one language somewhere in this world dies every fourteen days. It ceases to exist in its spoken form and, sometimes, in its written form too.

But a language never dies on its own. In most cases, dominant languages—those spoken with greater proficiency, especially those used for education and trade—take over, leaving the ones considered less important to vanish. People, too, choose to learn languages that give them better jobs and better lives for their families.

India is a country of oral traditions, where, since ancient times, communication across generations has mainly happened through folk songs and other spoken forms of storytelling. Even now, a huge fraction of India's population lives in remote and inaccessible parts of the country. And often, their languages are only spoken, that is, they do not have a written form. These languages are not recognized as official languages. They do not get any support from the central or state governments to grow amongst their own people. They are absent from official documents and from the education system, which forces these people to learn a language they don't know.

According to the 2011 census report, India, a country with a population of more than 1.4 billion people, has close to 800 languages and 19,500 dialects spoken as mother tongues. Yet, only twenty-two languages have been declared as official languages so far.

We have lost over 250 languages in the last fifty years in India alone. But where one language stops breathing, another is born elsewhere.

This book is an effort to bring the many stories behind some known and many unknown languages and scripts to readers. It is an attempt to give a voice to the languages that long to be heard, to be sung. In these pages, you will read stories about languages that will make you smile, make you happy, sad, and even proud. Because, while there are languages that are endangered—trying to survive in a world where languages like English and Hindi are growing in power—there are people devoting their lives to ensure that languages and the collective knowledge they hold survive.

Read about how early humans possibly communicated with each other and how the last speaker of the oldest Neolithic tribes of India gifted us a wealth of beautiful songs and stories. Know about the people of a village in Karnataka who speak Sanskrit as their first language and how a marginalized community created their own language to protect their identity.

And this is just the tip of the iceberg!

Join me as I embark on a linguistic journey to understand languages across the length and breadth of our country. I've selected a gentle violet for the cover of this book because it's also the colour of the highest sound frequency, which indicates that we're loud and clear about the fact that we want to do everything we can to preserve our languages from fading with time.

Brimming with mind-boggling mysteries, theories, discoveries, histories, and, above all, heart-warming and inspiring stories about our many tongues, this book promises to leave you tongue-tied.

Let's talk then, shall we?

CRRRRRRR CATRRRRRRR . . . the egg cracked. The celestial world trembled and shook. Thunder and lightning and all sorts of storms permeated the blue sky that now looked like a sea of grey.

Because this was no ordinary, boring, plain white egg and definitely not one you've seen or eaten. This was the *Hiranyagarbha* (*hiranya* means gold and *garbha* means womb or the egg in Sanskrit) or the golden cosmic egg! But what do you think came out of this cosmic egg? A fire-spitting dragon? An alien from outer space? A . . . er . . . chicken?

The answer is: none of the above. According to the Rig Veda, the Hiranyagarbha gave birth to the one and only Brahma. Lord Brahma. He created the entire universe but soon realized that it was chaotic: it lacked any kind of form, sense, or law and order.

So, Brahma decided to meditate and find an answer to this problem of cosmic proportions. He realized he needed help to organize this chaos. So, what did he do? Well, he simply created someone who could help him. Easy, isn't it? He made the entire universe after all; creating someone to organize it wouldn't be such a big deal for him.

Thus, Brahma created Goddess Saraswati. Some legends say that she was born from his mouth, and some say that she was born from his third eye as he meditated.

Saraswati gave us the sun, the moon, and the stars. She created the mountains and the valleys, the rivers, and the lakes. She created creatures, big and small to live in her creations. She created day and night and seasons. Saraswati completed what Brahma had started. She won over Brahma and the universe with her logic and intellect.

Brahma's universe was not chaotic anymore. There was order. There was structure. There was life. But soon, Brahma was faced with another crisis. If his universe was to function as one, its creatures had to communicate with each other.

How would the creatures understand each other?

How could they tell each other what they needed? How they felt?

Brahma thought a lot and soon found the answer to his questions in the idea of Vac Devi. Vagdevi or Goddess Vak or Vac Devi, one of the coolest avatars of Goddess Saraswati that resides on her tongue, was thus born.

If Saraswati meant knowledge, Vac gave that knowledge the power to express. Legend has it that she articulated thoughts and feelings, giving everyone a chance to express themselves. From Vedic hymns and powerful ritualistic chants to communication between ordinary creatures, she did it all. She was in the swishing of leaves, the thundering of clouds, the rolling of the stone, the chirruping of crickets, the twinkling of fireflies, the dance of the bees, the twittering of birds, the roar of wild cats, and the silence of the night.

Just like Vac Devi symbolizes the birth of speech, the stories in this section sow the seeds for the birth of languages—whether it's the origin of cave art, the birth of one of our ancestor languages, Sanskrit, or the discovery of the mother of all Indian scripts, Brahmi.

These stories will take you on a journey to the very beginning of how it all started . . .

LANGUAGE, NOT LANGUAGE

The Story behind Ancient Cave Art

Early humans are believed to have communicated in some form of language or another for more than 1,50,000 to 2,00,000 years. We, as a species, cannot live in isolation. We form communities and societies.

But how did our ancestors talk to each other?

Did they make sounds, like other animals do? Growl? Purr? Grunt?

Did they communicate in gestures? A sign language of sorts?

Did they speak languages, like we do?

While archaeologists, linguists, anthropologists, and various researchers have come up with numerous theories on how our ancestors communicated, no one can make concrete claims. We can only establish possible theories based on scientific analysis of the available evidence and our knowledge of languages as they are now.

While how it all began remains a mystery, what we do know is that early humans made paintings on the walls and ceilings of caves. And that they used this cave art to communicate with one another, perhaps leaving messages for future generations. Like us! And there's plenty of evidence in caves all over the world.

These early humans were hunter gatherers. They travelled in groups and used caves, which were nestled inside deep forests, as temporary shelters. The caves were warm and dry in winters and cool in summers. This, coupled with the abundance of food and water bodies providing a perennial supply of fresh water around the caves, made it an ideal choice as a temporary home for the hunters who wandered from one place to another for better sources of food and, later, for trade.

But these caves also ended up being the perfect canvas for these travellers to communicate with their families and friends who were left behind or who had perhaps lost their way.

This was the beginning of a brand-new way of recording day-to-day lives, experiences, thoughts, ideas, important messages, even entire cultures, and traditions. A way of speaking without actually speaking. A way of communicating without any sounds or gestures or being present at all!

Our ancestors discovered that they could make paint from the pigments available in natural objects like earth, leaves, twigs, water, among other things. They used limestone to make white paint and iron oxide to make red. They used manganese oxide and charcoal too. They powdered roots and vegetables, rocks, stones, leaves, and flowers and mixed them with animal fat, blood, or water. Then, they painted with their fingertips or with twigs and stems.

Everyone—children, women, and men—made handprints. The handprints were probably a way of telling future wanderers that someone had been in the cave before them.

They painted scenes from their daily lives. One can see art depicting hunters with intricate headgears, bows, quivers of arrows, and spears chasing big cats, bovids, wild boars, and even rhinos. There are paintings of women cooking food while children frolic around them. Some scenes depict large groups of people as well—celebrations, group dances, processions, battles, and much more.

These are not just line drawings. These are deep and detailed, and the real anatomy of the drawn objects is evident. The more developed cave paintings show movement in the animal and human figures too. Their bodies are sometimes larger than the head. They show fine details in the antlers and horns of animals such as the deer, rhino, and bison. Sometimes, they show animal and human figures together to show a comparison between their sizes!

They could depict a story or show how much knowledge our ancestors possessed. The art could have also been done during ceremonies and rituals that were practised in those times.

Wherever the early humans lived, there is cave art. It's no surprise that cave art is found all over the world, from Australia and Spain to France and China. Such rock shelter sites are also found all across India. The Bhimbetka Rock Shelters in Madhya Pradesh is the largest site with around 750 caves displaying rock art that's thousands of years old.

On a train journey from Bhopal to Itarsi, Dr Vishnu Wakankar, an archaeologist, saw the mighty Vindhya hills and instinctively thought they were historic and held some secrets. He got off at the next station on a whim and walked up to those hills only to find paintings in the very first cave he entered. This was in 1956 and, in 1957, Bhimbetka was introduced to the world.

The Bhimbetka Rock Shelters were declared a UNESCO World Heritage site in 2003.

Discovering the Bhimbetka caves was just the beginning of an illustrious career in archaeology for Dr Vishnu Wakankar. He discovered and recorded over 4000 painted caves in India alone. He studied caves across Europe, North America, and the Middle East. For his exemplary contribution in the discovery and study of cave art, Dr Wakankar is also known as the Pitamaha of Rock Art in India.

Languages are used to communicate, but can every tool that is used to communicate be called a language? Is cave art a language?

Cave art has elements of a language—action for verbs, objects for nouns, and descriptive art as adjectives. They are visual and symbolic. They were used to share information. They were used as recording diaries. These paintings made on cave walls and ceilings were used to mark the routes they took on their journey. Maybe they were imagined and fantasized scenes—the dreams our ancestors dreamed. Cave art tells us stories we would have perhaps never known.

But if only words could be fossilized! These cave paintings sadly give no indications if the early humans knew the words for the things they drew.

The cave art displayed no uniform structure or standardization. There was no consistency in the way they were done. Other than the paintings, archaeologists have found abstract symbols and codes, but none of them indicate a language.

Then why is this chapter here? Why talk about cave art at all?

Because we believe that maybe, just maybe, cave art was the origin of modern-day languages. That cave paintings were early signs of the creation of languages.

Some cave art may have been inspired by sounds—thundering roars, trotting hoofs, drumbeats, and songs. Or maybe cave paintings were just a way of decorating the cave shelters where our ancestors lived.

And even if all these theories hold no water, cave art tells us that our ancestors had the same cognitive abilities of processing information and communicating, like we do—they could think, deduce, analyse, and make sense of things around them.

The existence of cave art proves that we're all capable of communicating and building connections in a language of our own.

PITRA PATÉRA PATER

The Story of One of India's Ancestor Languages

Pitra Patéra Pater . . .

No. This is not the sound of the pitter patter of rain, nor is this a rhyme. They are the words for 'father' in Sanskrit, Greek, and Latin, respectively. Just like *trayas, treis, and tres* are the words for 'three'. And *bhratra, frater, frater,* for 'brother'. Or even *matr, metera, mater,* for 'mother' and *devas, theos, deus,* for 'god'. The list is endless, and these similarities are not a mere coincidence.

Sanskrit, just like Greek and Latin, is a descendent of the Indo-European languages. It has an extinct and unknown ancestor language known as Proto-Indo-European or PIE (where Proto means 'original' or 'earliest'). Linguists and researchers haven't been able to discover and reconstruct this extinct hypothetical language since it had no writing system. There's no evidence of what it possibly was.

The Indo-European languages are closely related and are widely spoken across Europe, the Americas, and southern Asia. When these languages travelled to the south of Asia, they interacted with earlier local languages to form the Indic or Indo-Aryan languages. This is where Sanskrit belongs.

The word Sanskrit comes from the word *samskrita*, which literally means 'perfected' or 'perfectly done'. But there's more to this language than just being one in which ancient texts, epics, or even our beloved Panchatantra stories have been written, thousands of years ago.

It's not just a language that only Hindu priests chant in. There are many villages in India where Sanskrit is spoken to communicate with one another: Jhiri, Bhaguwar, and Mohad in Madhya Pradesh, Sasana in Odisha, and Ganoda in Rajasthan.

But there is one village in Karnataka that takes the cake! In this sleepy hamlet, 300 km from Bengaluru, the state capital, everyone—from children to the elderly—knows how to speak, read, and write in Sanskrit. People here have been putting in extraordinary effort to preserve and keep this ancient language alive.

Located in Shivamogga district, along the fringes of the town of Shivamogga (Karnataka), is the village of Mattur, popularly known as the 'Sanskrit Village of India'. While the state language of Karnataka is Kannada, the primary language of the nearly 2000 people living in Mattur is Sanskrit.

In Mattur, one can see streets lined with green areca nut trees and lush paddy fields interspersed with colourful houses that are hundreds of years old. It is not uncommon to hear the sounds of children and grown-ups chanting Sanskrit shlokas alongside the chiming of temple bells.

Over 500 years ago, Sanskrit was only used to chant shlokas from the Vedas, and in religious discourses. But the people of Mattur are changing this. Thanks to some untiring individuals of this village with a passion for Sanskrit, the language is now used as a means of communicating, not just praying. They believe that until and unless a language is taught like a mother tongue, from birth, it's difficult to replace popular regional languages. In Mattur's case, Kannada or Sankethi, a dialect of Kannada, is also spoken there.

Organizations such as the Vishwa Sankethi Bharati (VSB) have been established to promote Sanskrit and Sankethi while keeping age-old Vedic traditions, classical music, and storytelling cultures such as the *gamaka* alive. They conduct language and culture courses that see students even from overseas.

The oldest form of Sanskrit is referred to as Vedic Sanskrit, the one in which our four Vedas (Rigveda, Yajurveda, Samaveda, Atharvaveda), Upanishads, and

Brahmanas have been composed, Rigveda being the foremost scripture. Where the Vedic period ended, the period of Classical Sanskrit began. If anyone says they know Sanskrit today, it means they know Classical Sanskrit—which is what the people of Mattur speak.

Students in many European countries, especially Germany, are learning Sanskrit as well. Many of them sign up for distant-learning courses with Sanskrit teachers from Mattur. Since some of the earliest human thoughts were written in Sanskrit, students are studying it to understand how minds worked in ancient times, and how ideas and cultures originated.

Sanskrit is also known as deva bhasha or the language of the gods, written in the Devanagari (script of the city of gods). Many say that Sanskrit is *apaurusheya,* which means 'not created by man', an eternal language with no beginning and no end. While it was considered a holy language, primarily used by the Brahmins, Lord Mahavira and Lord Buddha rejected caste hierarchy in society. They did not believe that only Brahmins held a prestigious position in society, and they never looked down upon other castes. They refused to use Sanskrit as their holy language. Instead, they used Prakrit languages—the natural languages of expression of the masses, especially Pali, for writing scriptures.

Many myths and legends surround this ancient language. Some say when Panini, the insatiable scholar, grammarian, and linguist, was in penance to attain more knowledge, Shiva played his damaru to wake him up, producing fourteen sounds. These sounds echoed in his ears, and he used them to compile the grammatical rules of Sanskrit and wrote them in eight chapters known as *Ashtadhyayi* or *Eight Chapters*. This highly structured book of grammar is relevant even today. It's a little wonder why he is not only the Father of Sanskrit but the Father of Indian Linguistics.

Ashtadhyayi is an ancient, yet elegant, sophisticated, systematic, and scientific book of grammar written in about 4000 verses that makes Sanskrit a language that does not change on its own over time, like other languages we know of. But it's language that can infinitely accommodate more and more words as time goes by and as human cultures evolve, without affecting or changing the core language at all! Sanskrit has a mindboggling number of words and is a constantly evolving language, with newer Sanskrit words being coined even today! Each word has many synonyms, thus making the language that much richer and easier to understand from various perspectives.

OFFICIAL LANGUAGES OF INDIA

ASSAMESE
BENGALI
GUJARATI
HINDI
KANNADA
KASHMIRI
KONKANI
MALAYALAM
MANIPURI
MARATHI
NEPALI

ORIYA
PUNJABI
SANSKRIT
SINDHI
TAMIL
TELUGU
URDU
BODO
SANTHALI
MAITHILI
DOGRI

India has twenty-two official languages. These languages are used for oral and written communication by the union government for administrative purposes, along with English. They are listed in the Eighth Schedule of our Constitution. The government works towards the growth and development of these languages. Sanskrit is not only one of these twenty-two official languages of India, but is also the second official language of Uttarakhand and Himachal Pradesh, and one of the six Classical Indian languages. A Classical Indian language is an ancient language with a recorded history of more than 1500 years, one whose literature possesses heritage value that's not borrowed from any other language, and whose classical form of literature is very distinct from modern-day texts. Kannada, Malayalam, Odia, Tamizh (Tamil) and Telugu are our other Classical languages.

Sanskrit speakers in India constitute only 0.00198 per cent of our entire population, yet, in 2018, India recorded over 24,000 Sanskrit speakers, a rise of more than 10,000 speakers since 2011. And villages like Mattur are leading the way, showing the rest of the country that it's not rocket science to learn ancestor languages like Sanskrit and use it in day-to-day conversations. In fact, it's even cool to learn an ancestor language, in which lie the roots of early human thoughts, ideology, and culture.

१

BORN TO PROTECT
The Story of Hijras and Their Secret Language

In the fifteenth century, during the Mughal era, hijras were appointed as protectors of queens and kings. They were advisors in Mughal courts. They were looked upon as having special godly powers, or *baraka,* which means 'blessing' in Urdu and in Arabic, and their blessings were sought during auspicious occasions such as marriages or the birth of a baby. Hijras even rode fine horses and wore dazzling attire, fit for royals. They lived in palatial homes and had servants attending to them.

Much before that, hijras have been spoken about in Hindu epics such as the Ramayana and the Mahabharata. An avatar of Lord Shiva, Ardhanari, in which Shiva merges with his wife, Parvati, is a deity that the hijras worship. Even Lord Vishnu and Goddess Lakshmi merge to form one deity known as Vaikuntha-Kamalaja or Lakshmi-Narayan. Krishna, too, had taken the form of a woman known as Mohini, to marry Aravan, the son of the mighty Pandava warrior, Arjun.

Hijras were highly respected in Hindu mythology and held prominent positions in Mughal courts. However, when the British came to India, they ostracized the hijras from being a part of the mainstream 'binary' society—where individuals are registered as female or male at birth—because hijras cannot be classified as strictly females or strictly males.

Most hijras are either born as males or as intersex children, meaning those who are born with physical attributes that are different from conventional females and males. Hijras grow up and live as females in the way they feel, think, behave, and dress.

While this was a normal way of life for the hijras, the British neither understood them nor accepted them. The British stigmatized the hijra community as one that clearly did not belong to the larger society. They created a special act (Criminal Tribes Act of 1871) under which hijras could be imprisoned without any reason and be charged for criminal offenses they were not guilty of. Anything they said was held against them. For the very first time, the hijras were forced to go underground and live separately in hiding.

Did you know that it's not abnormal to be born as an intersex child? According to the UN, nearly 1.7 per cent of

children across the world are born as intersex children. In India alone, at least 10,000 intersex children are born each year. They are normal individuals, like everyone else, and they don't need to 'change' or become 'normal' to fit into a standard world. We need to change the way we look at them, be kind to them, and accept them as one of us.

This unfair treatment by the British sparked the need for a language only they could understand. A language that could protect them from imprisonment, abuse, and violent treatment.

This secret language of the hijras is known as Hijra Farsi among the Muslim hijras of the Indian subcontinent (India, Pakistan, Bangladesh) and Gupti language or Ulti Bhasha among the Hindu hijras. This language is only known to the hijras who speak it. Historically, there have been secret languages spoken by the trans communities in the Western world, but they are now extinct because those communities have seen more acceptance and they do not feel the need to communicate in codes anymore.

Hijra Farsi or the Gupti language is not a new language; it has been spoken since the fifteenth century, during the Mughal period. There is no known connection between Hijra Farsi and Arabic languages. Hijra Farsi was developed during the Mughal era, when Persian was spoken, hence it came to be known as Hijra Farsi.

Hijras learn this language only after they are christened as being a part of the mainstream hijra community. When new hijras enter the community, they learn the code language from the guru or leader, and they become chelas or followers. They not only speak a different language, but their way of talking is also different. They mimic their gurus and the other senior members of the guru-chela community and learn the language through listening and through practise. The language remains a secret language because speakers are few and the sources from which they learn the language stay within the community itself. But it's knowing this secret language that makes one a true hijra and gives them an identity of their own.

But how does speaking a different language help their community?

Hijras feel that using a different language is a natural progression of exploring and expressing their identities. Since they are an underprivileged minority and a marginalized community where groups of individuals are treated as insignificant or non-existent, they are often suppressed and subjected to ill treatment and social taboos. They use their language in public places so that no one can understand them or judge them for who they are. Over time, the community has realized that it's their language that has united them and given them the sense of belonging to one another when everyone else has treated them as social outcasts—many of them have been abandoned by their families only because they are unlike them. This code language constantly evolves by itself and lends itself as a powerful tool that keeps their lives secret from those who want to cause them harm. It is a tool that is used to show solidarity towards their entire community.

Secret languages are not a new phenomenon in India. Code languages have always existed in different societies—whether they are individuals or communities, or intelligence agencies. For instance, Mygurudu is a secret language or argot made by simply interchanging Malayalam letters. It was used by the Malabari people of Kerala, who were imprisoned by the British in 1921. This language helped the individuals communicate among themselves around other prison inmates and prison security guards.

There are enough research papers and sufficient evidence to prove that Hijra Farsi and Gupti languages are indeed complete languages and not just a bunch of secret words layered upon an existing language to form one. They have a unique vocabulary and follow a particular grammar and syntax, replete with all the elements of a language—nouns, verbs, adjectives, parts of a speech and so on. They even have their own words for numbers, mainly for various denominations of currency! For instance, *dasola*

is ten, *adhi vadvi* is fifty, *vadvi* is hundred, *panj vadvi* is five hundred and so on.

Hijra Farsi has more than 10,000 words, including some borrowed words from other languages such as Hindi and Urdu. These borrowed words depend on where the hijras are located geographically. For instance, in Mumbai, they may borrow from Hindi, Marathi and Urdu, and, in Karachi, they may borrow from Urdu and Pashto. It doesn't have any written script or dialects.

Even today, the hijra community is underprivileged and extremely poor, chiefly because they are not considered as a part of mainstream society and are not allowed to enjoy the same privileges. They struggle for basic human rights such as healthcare, housing, employment, and education, which is why many of them turn to begging to make ends meet. They are abused as a community and, at times, they have to deal with violence too. All of this has threatened their survival.

But Hijra Farsi is that sliver of hope for this community. An increasing number of hijras are learning this language that ties them together, protects and empowers them. It is amazing how a language can bring with it a sense of identity, security, and pride; something a banished community can call their own and only their own— the hijra's very own survival tool, secret weapon, and perhaps a bandage to heal their many wounds.

THREE HEROES AND A PASSER-BY

The Story of the Mother of All Indian Scripts

When we are talking of languages, the story of the written systems of languages cannot be far behind.

This is the story of three young heroes and a passer-by belonging to very different time periods. They gave the world one of the most precious gifts—the mother of all Indian scripts, from which every modern Indian script and several scripts in Southeast Asia have been derived. This is the story of the Brahmi script.

Did you know that only those languages that have a written script are given the official status of a language? The rest are classified as dialects or other forms of languages.

Circa Second Century BCE

War after war. Conquest after conquest. Young Ashoka fought bloody battles when he ascended the throne of the Mauryan Empire in 260 BCE to spread the empire as far and wide as he could. And he succeeded in his mission. The Mauryan Empire extended from Iran in the east to Burma in the west, from the Himalayas in the north to the southern plateaus of India.

But while waging wars, little did he realize that he was waging an internal battle with his conscience that was unable to handle all the bloodshed and destruction. The Kalinga war in 270 BCE marked the end of Ashoka's violent military adventures. The death of nearly three lakh people in the war broke Ashoka completely. He vowed to never raise a weapon, to never wage a war, to never kill anything, not even an insect.

A new King Ashoka was born. An awakened king who gave up violence, adopted Buddhism and embarked on the path of ahimsa or non-violence, just like his grandfather, Chandragupta Maurya, who became a Jain monk.

An enlightened Ashoka didn't just adopt Buddhism, he propagated it—its virtues, its teachings, its doctrines. He carved his ideas and thoughts—messages of peace, love, compassion and truth, and the path to *dhamma* (dharma), which are the fundamental principles of a rightful way of life—on rocks, caves, and pillars. These carved pillars, known as edicts, were erected in all parts of his kingdom, even as far away as Iran, Afghanistan, Pakistan, and Sri Lanka. These inscriptions were in Prakrit languages, local derivatives of Sanskrit. The most amazing thing was that each of the edicts was written in a form of Prakrit specific to the region in which it was erected, allowing locals to understand them. He wanted generations of people to read them, and hopefully, follow them too. He used one script in the Indian subcontinent, while the edicts in the far north-west were written in Greek and Aramaic languages, in a script known as Kharosthi.

Little did Ashoka know that these Brahmi inscriptions would inspire every writing system in the Indian subcontinent thereafter.

Time went by. Generations came and went. The Brahmi script was lost to the world and soon forgotten.

Then, along came a passer-by, nearly 1000 years later.

Circa Fourteenth Century CE

Delhi was now ruled by Feroz Shah Tughlaq. He was enamoured by the Ashoka stambhs or pillars that were erected at Topra-Kalan in Haryana and in Meerut. Even though he had no idea what was written on the pillars and who had built and erected them there, he thought those tall and beautiful pillars would look absolutely royal in Delhi. He wanted to take them back with him.

And so he did. Feroz Shah Tughlaq took two pillars back with him, now known as the Delhi-Topra pillar and the Delhi-Meerut pillar. The pillars were sent by boat and carted all the way to the capital city. The ornate pillars stood there as pieces of decoration for many years without a clue of what they truly represented.

We must wait almost 500 years for another hero to come by.

Circa Eighteenth Century CE

The East India Company had firmly established themselves in the country. They had won battles, made deals with the local rulers, and found a home. But they knew little about India's ancient history. Soon, British scholars, authors, poets, and researchers started coming to India with a keen interest in its rich past.

One of these scholars was a certain James Prinsep, who studied ancient artifacts. At the age of twenty, he joined Calcutta Mint, where coins were minted, or manufactured to be used as currency. The quality of the material—gold, silver, and copper—was tested.

As an employee at the Calcutta Mint, he started looking at ancient Indian coins and the inscriptions on them. He tried hard but couldn't decipher what was written on them. And it wasn't just coins. He came across several inscribed rocks, stones, and pillars from across India and even Sri Lanka.

Then he saw the pillars in Delhi.

The same script! He was flummoxed. What could these inscriptions be? James started to study all the inscriptions together—the rocks, the coins, the pillars. The more he studied them, the more he identified similarities between them. Some inscriptions on the pillars were even identical! Two words kept repeating themselves in most of the edicts—'Devanampiya Piyadasi'.

James was persistent. He tried all he could and finally, the moment for which he had worked such a long time arrived in 1837. A historian from Sri Lanka informed him that 'Piyadasi' was the assumed name of none other than King Ashoka, who called himself 'Beloved of the Gods'.

Everything started to fall into place. The letters and words he had been studying all along started to speak to him. James Prinsep had done what nobody had—he deciphered the messages that Ashoka wanted to share with the world.

The Brahmi script greeted the world, and nothing was the same ever again. It was discovered that many scripts were born from the Brahmi script—such as the rounded south Indian scripts or the more angular north Indian scripts. Brahmi was also the ancestor script for Southeast Asian scripts such as the Javanese script of Indonesia, the Khmer script of Cambodia, and the Mon script of Burma.

Our heroes, Ashoka the Great and James Prinsep, and our passer-by, Feroz Shah Tuglaq, knowingly or unknowingly, gave our country an ancestor script.

But who's the third hero?

Circa Twenty-first Century CE

Nearly 200 years later, the world was now driven by technology at its helm. In India, languages are a major hurdle for a majority of the population, who cannot read or write in English. They are unable to use most of the applications and services that smartphones offer. But our third hero solved this problem.

The third hero is not a human but a keyboard—the Indic keyboard.

It's a keyboard that supports twenty-three Indian languages based on the Brahmi script! It can be installed on mobile phones and can be used to type anything—emails, texts, social media posts, and so on. Indians can now connect with others in their native languages from their phones without having to worry if they know how to read or write in English.

Newer generations of Indians who know how to speak, read, or write their mother tongues and regional languages are dwindling, and we must constantly endeavour to keep our languages and our writing systems alive. For we never know if a King Ashoka, a Feroz Shah Tughlaq or a James Prinsep will be reborn to revive them again.

4

POOL OF TAATAi AT PERUTERUR

The Story of Some of India's Oldest Written Evidence

Nestled among dense forests and big and small hills in ancient Tamil Nadu, in the vicinity of present-day towns such as Madurai, Tiruvannamalai, and Kanchipuram, are caves that have some stories to tell. These hills are treacherous to climb. And once you manoeuvre them through steep ridges that demand some serious rock-climbing abilities and the determination to make it to the top, you will find yourself at the mouth of dark and mysterious caves. Many of these caves have a freshwater spring, waterfall or even a water body either along the foothills of the caves or at the top. While you may encounter an occasional family of bats that's woken up from its day-time siesta, the light shining on the walls of the caves through cracks and crevices reveal a piece of history that dates to around 300 BCE.

In the caves of Mangulam or Kalugumalai, Alagarmalai, Samanarmalai, where *malai* means 'hill' or 'mountain', are inscriptions in the Tamil-Brahmi script, the oldest of which dates back to around second century BCE. These inscriptions talk about a flourishing Jain culture in south India.

Today, the Jain community is the smallest of the six major religious groups in India, constituting only about 0.4 per cent of the entire Indian population. While most of the community are found in the states of Maharashtra, Gujarat, and Rajasthan, only around 25,000 to 30,000 are Tamil Jains. However, this is a miniscule number compared to the thriving Tamil Jain population thousands of years ago.

Around 298 BCE, Chandragupta Maurya, the founder of the Mauryan dynasty, renounced his throne and become a Jain ascetic. He became a follower of the revered Jain monk, Acharya Bhadrabahu, who had predicted a widespread famine in north India. To avoid this impending famine, Acharya Bhadrabahu left with his disciples, including Chandragupta Maurya, for the south. They migrated to Shravanabelagola, a very popular Jain pilgrimage site in present-day Karnataka, where the seeds for Jainism in the south of India were sown. From there, they moved further south to ancient Tamil Nadu, also known as the Tamilakam or Tamizhagam, a much larger Tamil Nadu, which included Kerala and the old state of Madurai.

Soon, the Jain dharma and way of life spread among Tamil Nadu. It influenced Tamil culture, religion, politics, and society at large. Just like the Buddhists, the Tamil Jain monks converted caves into monasteries and used them for meditation and for shelter during monsoon. Inside these caves, there are stone beds, or berths with raised stone pillows. Each of these beds is named after the Jain monks who occupied them or the sculptors who carved them. At the entrance of many of the caves are nuanced monolithic carvings of Jain Tirthankaras or Jain spiritual teachers such as Adinath, Parshwanath, and Mahavira. These inscriptions are valuable discoveries that help in the study of Jainism in ancient Tamil Nadu and throw light on Tamil culture and language.

IRobert Sewell, a civil servant and Indologist—someone who studies Indian culture, history, and literature—at the Madras Presidency during the British period, discovered the first Tamil inscriptions at the Mangulam caves in 1882. As an in-charge of the Archaeology Department, he was entrusted with the job of finding ancient inscriptions and epigraphs in that region.

Did you know that one of the reasons the British took up excavations across the country was to unearth our hidden

histories and position themselves as the only people who could help us understand our past better?

When epigraphist—someone who studies ancient carvings and inscriptions— and historian K.V. Subrahmanya Aiyar came to know of these, he recognized that the sounds of the inscribed letters belonged to the Tamil language. And that the language in the inscriptions had been adapted to incorporate the local and regional variants of Tamil phonetics. He also realized that the script was similar to the Brahmi script from the Ashokan period. He aptly called this the Tamil-Brahmi script, also known as Tamili or Damili.

Later, the very talented and remarkable civil servant turned epigraphist, Iravatham Mahadevan, would record the data on the inscriptions and date the Mangulam inscriptions to the second century BCE.

For example, one inscription in the Mangulam caves has the name of King Nedunchezhiyan I, a king from the Pandya dynasty who is known to have ruled from around 270 BCE, among the names of other kings and Jain monks.

An inscription at Samanarmalai, another Jain *palli* or monastery, reads:

peruterur uzhi taatai ay-am

This translates to Pool of Taatai at Peruterur, where Taatai means 'father', *ay-am* means pool or spring or waterfall, and Peruterur is perhaps the former name of a village.

Alongside the cave inscriptions, stones, seals, coins, and pottery sherds inscribed in ancient Tamil, dating as early as the second century BCE, have been found at excavation sites in India, Oman, Thailand, Sri Lanka, and Egypt.

So many details emerge from deciphering inscriptions. In the case of Tamil or Tamizh, the archaeological written evidence suggests that the various dynasties that ruled Tamil Nadu in ancient India such as the Kalabhras, Pandyas, Pallavas, Cheras, and Cholas, had trade relations with people in the Far East and Europe, right up to Greece and Rome. They also suggest that Tamizh was a proper spoken and written language, and that the traders and businesspersons were literate and educated.

This makes inscriptions undoubtedly valuable written records of literate human life in ancient times. They provide strong evidence about the cultural and linguistic landscape of the era to which they belong. They give us deep insight into ancient dynasties, how life was lived and how civilizations and languages have evolved over time. They could be names of kings and queens or traders, food people ate, the animals and birds that existed in those times, and so much more.

But the exponential rate at which urbanization has spread across the country has left many important excavation sites with inscriptions vulnerable and in a state of pity. Like Nala Sopara, a suburb on the outskirts of Mumbai, which was once one of the largest, most prosperous trading ports on the west coast of India. From remains of Ashokan rock edict inscriptions in the Brahmi script that go back over 2500 years and Buddhist stupas to fragments of Buddha's begging bowl, Nala Sopara is abundant with objects that point to a rich past. Archaeologists believe that there are still more significant discoveries to be made in and around Nala Sopara.

But despite being declared as a protected national site by the Government of India and being managed by the Archaeological Survey of India (ASI), there are so many ruins there that lie in various stages of damage.

Did you know that the branch of epigraphy (the study of ancient written inscriptions and records) and numismatics (the study of coins and currency) of the ASI has been in existence since 1887 and is headquartered in Mysore? They have explored the length and breadth of the country and discovered epigraphs dating as far back as the second century BCE.

Most ancient objects that are being excavated have some or the other form of inscription on them. They could be patterns, symbols, letters, or pictographic elements. But there's a lot more to them than meets the eye because they all mean something in some language, acting like time-travelling machines that help us go back thousands of years and find out information about the past that can be critical to understand our present. We need to make sincere efforts to protect and preserve them because they hold the many stories behind ancient kingdoms and the secrets behind our ancestral tapestry that we may never know if they are not studied.

The Vijayanagara Empire (present-day Hampi in north Karnataka) was ruled by one of the most able, powerful, and thoughtful rulers India has ever seen—Krishna Deva Raya of the Tuluva dynasty.

The people of Vijayanagara loved their emperor. In the two decades that he reigned over this kingdom, he brought it peace and prosperity, unlike the kings before him.

While he remained undefeated in the many battles he fought during his reign, what Krishna Deva Raya loved more than anything else was literature and languages. He was a poet and a scholar himself. He had immense respect for all languages. His court had distinguished scholars and poets who spoke Sanskrit, Tulu, Kannada, Telugu, and Tamizh, including the wise Tenali Ramakrishna or Tenali Rama. Tenali was one of the *Ashtadiggajas* or eight great poets and scholars of this court.

These celebrated scholars wrote some of the most notable literary works and poetry of the time. Throughout his reign, Deva Raya praised and encouraged them to create more literature. Even though Telugu flourished in his kingdom—his period is also known as the Golden Period for Telugu literature—he patronized several Kannada, Tamizh, Sanskrit, and Tulu writers and poets. Deva Raya himself wrote in Telugu and Sanskrit with equal ease and flair.

There was no official language in Vijayanagara—Telugu, Kannada and Sanskrit were widely spoken. People enjoyed a democratic way of life. Everyone in his kingdom was free to speak and write in their languages, as well as practise their respective cultures and traditions.

All these languages got a chance to flourish only because an able ruler loved his subjects and languages enough to support and encourage their use. And just like these languages, thousands of languages across the world have evolved and adapted due to a multitude of reasons—population migration, invasions, colonization, and so on. But those languages that did not receive any acknowledgement or patronage from their governments, met undesirable fates, some of them perishing without a trace.

Entire populations and cultures have been wiped out and continue to lose their voice due to the loss of languages. The increasing gap between the dominant languages, those that enjoy the administration's support, and the dominated languages, those that are suppressed and led to obscurity, has given rise to linguistic apartheid or discrimination.

It's imperative to understand that languages make us human. And the more diverse our languages, the richer our cultures, the more collective knowledge of our natural ecosystems and biodiversity stays with us for generations. Just like Krishna Deva Raya, we need able administrators who respect and patronize diverse languages and encourage learning and literature in mother languages.

The stories in this section paint a portrait of how languages change and grow into different versions of themselves over time, and how each one of them enrich and contribute towards our linguistic diversity.

THE CASE OF LINGUISTIC BOUNDARIES

The Story of India's State Reorganization Act

We fought hard for our freedom from British rule. And soon a day arrived when the hopes, dreams, and sacrifices of millions of Indians bore fruit—the British were finally forced to leave India. But while there was exhilaration and celebration everywhere, there was tension and stress in the meeting of the Indian National Congress (INC).

'The problem of the states is so difficult that *you* alone can solve it,' said Gandhiji, breaking the silence in the room. No one had a clue on how to stop India from breaking into hundreds of fragments. The British had created almost six hundred princely states under their regime and now that the British were headed back, these princely states were looking for an opportunity to declare themselves as independent states. India being partitioned into India and Pakistan was another looming problem.

Vallabhbhai Patel looked up. All eyes were on him. He was well aware that reuniting India would be a monumental, nearly impossible, task to accomplish. But the thought that India would lose what made it so unique—the diverse ethnicities, cultures, traditions, languages, and geographic distribution—was agonizing. National security and stability were also at risk and for Vallabhbhai Patel, people came first. Their security and prosperity were paramount.

But why would it be so difficult to unite India, to unite all those princely states into one single country? Now, all these states were diverse in the way they were created and run. Some were too big while the others were too small. While some were created based on historic traditions, some for administrative convenience, others were based on ethnic similarities in specific regions. But largely, all of them were created for some political gain or another for the British. Even though they were headed by local princes, they all had to report to the British government.

The Congress established the States Department for the first time in 1947 to ensure that all the princely states joined India. The job of unifying these states into the Indian dominion or region was in the able hands of the very astute Vallabhbhai Patel, with V.P. Menon as his secretary.

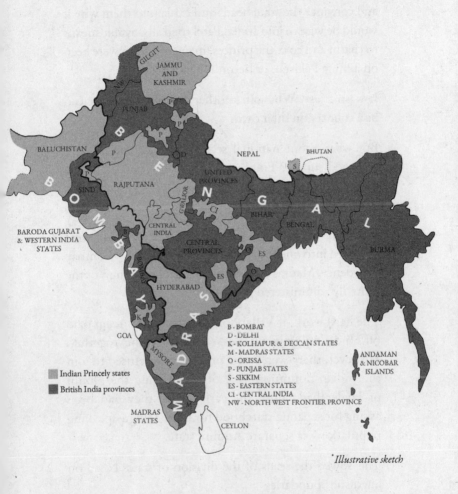

The Bengal province, the Bombay province and the Madras province of British India

As a team, they worked round the clock to call, cajole, and convince the state heads and explain to them why it would be wise to join India. Patel tried all possible means to charm and coax the princes, many of whom were keen on joining Pakistan or becoming independent.

It wasn't easy. Why join another country when one can be a country on their own?

But what about national security and defence? Water and food supply? Employment? Healthcare? Economic growth? Administrative concerns?

Not all princely states were self-sufficient in the way they were run and hence most states acceded and were absorbed into one Indian province or another—Bombay Presidency, Madras Presidency, Bengal Presidency, or the centrally administered provinces.

The hard work of Vallabhbhai Patel and his team paid off. India's jigsaw puzzle started to come together. However, there were some princes who refused to join the Indian dominion, one of them being the Nizam of Hyderabad. Since the early 1920s, they had been asking for separate statehood for their Telugu-speaking population—a separate Andhra state.

This sowed the seeds of the division of states based on linguistic boundaries.

At that time, there was complete consensus that it was best to decide state boundaries based on languages. This had its own advantages—better communication between people, improved education, easier trade practices, and effective governance.

For once, regional languages would get a boost. Literature and arts in those languages would flourish. One's language is also associated with a set of culture and traditions, shared lives and experiences. The bond that people speaking one language share is significant. It was thought to be best to have one language in one state to promote peace, harmony, and progress among its populace.

But Prime Minister Jawaharlal Nehru was never really for it. He knew that while this system supported a linguistic majority, it also gave rise to linguistic minorities. He believed such a division based on languages would work only if majority of the population of that region was in agreement.

With the British leaving the country and the creation of Pakistan leaving behind a post-Partition refugee crisis, the security and safety of the people in the Indian subcontinent were at stake. They had just managed to unify and merge the princely states into India, a country that had already been divided based on religious ethnicities. How could they further divide it based on languages?

This wasn't done. It just wasn't the right time for the formation of linguistic provinces. Nehru was only being practical about the whole situation. At one of the legislative assemblies, he said, 'First things must come first, and the first thing is the security and stability of India.'

In view of his concerns, the Linguistic Provinces Commission, also known as the Dar Commission, was set up to revisit the proposals for creating Andhra, Kerala, Karnataka, and Maharashtra based on the common language spoken there. After careful reviews, the commission declared that administrative convenience, financial health, geographical contiguity, and prosperity of its people, and not languages must be the primary parameters for considering the creation of any separate state.

The JVP Committee, which comprised of Jawaharlal Nehru, Vallabhbhai Patel, and Dr Pattabhi Sitaramaya, was appointed to review the looming demand of separation based on languages. While the committee kept citing more realistic reasons for state reorganization rather than languages, there were many who did not agree with them.

The Madras Presidency was multilingual. It had Telugu, Tamizh, Kannada, Malayalam, and Oriya. The Telugu-speaking people always felt that the Tamizh-speaking population received preferential treatment and wanted a separate state in a bid to preserve their culture.

One person put up a clear fight for the sake of his Telugu community. He was none other than Potti Sriramulu, a very devout yet lesser-known freedom fighter.

Born in Nellore that was part of the Madras Presidency, Sriramulu was an engineering graduate who worked with the Railways. He was an active freedom fighter who chiefly fought for the rights of the less fortunate.

At twenty-five, after losing his child, wife, and mother, he renounced material life and joined the Sabarmati Ashram. He was a staunch Gandhian and fought alongside Gandhiji in the Quit India Movement and the Salt Satyagraha. He was very empathetic towards the suffering of the poor and devoted his life to their service. He fasted for their basic rights.

The Congress had been delaying the creation of the Andhra state for a very long time. Many protestors fasted in solidarity, but it did not move the government.

Sriramulu started a fast unto death for the state of Andhra on 19 October 1952. For weeks, the government did not respond. Nehru believed that if they kept giving in to such protests, India would not be a democracy anymore.

But Sriramulu did not stop his fasting like the others had so far. He fasted for over two months! His health had completely deteriorated. But Sriramulu did not concede. On 15 December 1952, the fifty-eighth day of his fasting, Sriramulu passed away.

Hundreds of people joined his death procession. Riots broke out. Public property was damaged. People were not willing to let Sriramulu's sacrifice go to vain.

The uproar did not die. Seven people lost their lives to police firing. Life was disrupted in the Madras Presidency and in three days following Sriramulu's death, on 19 December 1952, Jawaharlal Nehru granted independent statehood to the Telugu-speaking population. Thus, Andhra Pradesh was born.

When the state of Andhra Pradesh was created from Hyderabad, the people of the Telangana region were unhappy even though they were Telugu speakers. They claimed that not enough attention was paid to oversee Telangana's development and, therefore, they demanded a separate Telangana state. While the State Reorganization Committee (SRC) recommended that a separate Telangana state be created, the Congress denied it. Instead, the regions of Andhra and Telangana signed a Gentleman's Agreement where it was agreed that even though Telangana would be a part of Andhra Pradesh, the interests of its people would be safeguarded. However, that did not happen and in 2014, Telangana was finally born.

Sriramulu's death had marked the birth of a new India map that would be redrawn based on linguistic lines. Old borders were erased. New borders were redrawn keeping in mind the nation's welfare, security, sense of unity, integrity, and economic prosperity.

The first of May is celebrated as Maharashtra Day every year, for it was on this day in 1960 that the Bombay Reorganization Act was passed, and the Bombay state was split into the states of Maharashtra and Gujarat. When states were being reorganized, there was tension in the erstwhile Bombay state where a distinct population spoke Marathi and Konkani and the other significant half of the population spoke Gujarati and Kutchhi. Each group of people wanted their own independent state—a multilingual state with Bombay as the capital city was not working. There were protests across Bombay. Sadly, in one of the protests at Hutatma Chowk, the police fired at the peaceful protestors. 107 protestors were killed. Subsequently, the government gave in and on 1 May 1960, Maharashtra and Gujarat were separated based on linguistic lines.

There were many concerns regarding the reorganization of states based on languages, the most important being that people wouldn't feel a sense of national unity if they were divided on the basis of languages. That patriotism towards one's own language and culture would overshadow patriotic feelings towards the country at large. Also, if a person from one state moved to another state for any reason, say employment, and continued to live there, their homeland would still be their home state. It was possible that such people would be treated with hostility in the new state, as someone who did not belong to the community or culture. Administrative, financial, economic, and geographic concerns were already discussed.

But public sentiment for having linguistic boundaries was so strong that state reorganization based on languages was an inevitable eventuality. The Congress succumbed to the pressures of popular demand and in the years following 1956, India was divided into fourteen major states and six union territories. At present (as of 2022), India has twenty-eight states and eight union territories.

Today, an increasing number of states are becoming multilingual as people are migrating across states; education, better livelihoods and an improved quality of life being the prime reasons. They are learning new languages to adapt to newer geographies. This intermix of different languages has led to language shifts where languages borrow words from each other over time to create new languages. The feeling of pride towards the dominant state language is slowly evaporating.

Will linguistic boundaries hold true in the future? Will India see a new state reorganization?

Only time will tell.

Did you know that Indian currency notes have a language panel on the reverse side of the note, where the denomination is written in fifteen of the twenty-two official languages of India? These languages are Assamese, Bengali, Gujarati, Kannada, Kashmiri, Konkani, Malayalam, Marathi, Nepali, Oriya, Punjabi, Sanskrit, Tamil, Telugu, and Urdu, in that order.

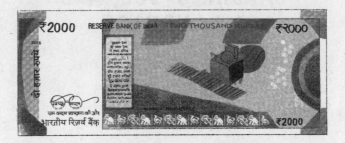

Reverse face of a Rs 2000 currency note

GANDHi, GODSE, AND A LANGUAGE
The Story of Hindustani, Hindi, and Urdu

Have you heard of anyone being assassinated for supporting a language?

Let's go back to twelfth-century India. Historically, there was a different language spoken by people in and around Delhi (north-west India) and that language was known as 'Hindustani'.

The Mughals arrived in India in the early thirteenth century. Among many other things like paintings, architecture and arts, they brought with them Persian, Arabic, and Turkic words that were soon absorbed in the local Hindustani language. Thus, a hybrid mix of multiple languages, that eased communication between people, was born.

A part of India's population introduced more Sanskrit words to their Hindustani language and wrote in the Devanagari script, which is the script in which Sanskrit is written. This came to be known as Hindi. Another part of the Indian population introduced more Persian and Arabic words to the language and wrote in the Nasta'liq script, which is a variation of the Arabic calligraphy style (in fact, quite different from Arabic). This language became Urdu. Thus, the sibling languages, Hindi and Urdu, were born from Hindustani. Linguists do not consider Hindi and Urdu as two separate languages. They are the same languages with same grammar where only higher literary words are different.

Many conquests by Muslim rulers, including Alauddin Khilji, Malik Kafur, and Muhammad Tugluq, happened in the south-west of India in the thirteenth century. With them, many Muslim families shifted from Delhi in the north to the Deccan in the south, which was inhabited by the Maharashtrians, Telugus, Tulus, and Kannadigas. When these Mughal rulers travelled southwards, their Persian language also travelled with them, but it did not stay the same.

Then came the rebellious Alauddin Hasan Bahman Shah, a Turkish general in the Mughal dynasty, in 1347.

He left the Mughals in Delhi to go south and form his own dynasty, also known as the Bahmani kingdom (1347–1518). He fought wars with the neighbouring Hindu rulers, especially the Vijayanagara empire, and formed new states—Ahmednagar, Bijapur, Golconda, and Bidar.

This was the Muslim kingdom of the Deccan region, the plateau region of south-west India that extended from the Arabian Sea in the west to the Bay of Bengal in the east, with Gulbarga as its capital.

As time went by and different communities co-existed, the languages fused together to form Dakhni. It's a harmonious blend of Persian, Hindustani, Marathi, Telugu, and Kannada vocabularies.

Soon, people in the Deccan region began to speak Dakhni. Sufi saints wrote poetry or *namas* in Dakhni and literary works in Dakhni were produced. The Dakhni language is spoken even now in cities such as Hyderabad, Mumbai, Bidar, Gulbarga, Mysore and other places in Maharashtra, Andhra Pradesh, Telangana, Karnataka, and even Tamil Nadu.

While Dakhni has never been listed in the official language census of India, and no one claims Dakhni as their mother tongue, crores of people are estimated to speak in Dakhni daily.

Urdu, one of the most charming, elegant, and eloquent of languages, is an Indo-Aryan language, just like Hindi; it's Hindi with a higher literary vocabulary. It's the eleventh most widely spoken language in the world. There are seventy million people who speak Urdu as a first language and 100 million who speak Urdu as a second language. As per the 2011 census, in India alone, more than 50 million people speak Urdu. The Constitution of India recognizes Urdu as one of its twenty-two official languages. It is also one of the official state languages in New Delhi, Kashmir, Uttar Pradesh, Bihar, West Bengal, and Telangana.

Did you know that while Urdu is the national language of Pakistan, only about 8 per cent of Pakistani citizens speak Urdu as their first language?

Linguistic diversity flourished over time. People spoke in Hindustani, Hindi, Urdu, Dakhni and other variants of the same language. But the government felt the need to unite our vast country with a single language. Soon, the quest for an official language began.

Post-Independence, the government of India debated on what our official language should be. Urdu had been declared as the national language of Pakistan. Hindi topped the list for India. But there was someone who was against Hindi becoming the official language of India—Gandhiji.

Gandhiji loved learning languages. He was a master of his mother tongue, Gujarati, but he learned other languages to communicate with more people and serve them better. He had learned Urdu while working with the Muslims in South Africa, and Tamizh while working with the labourers in Madras (now Chennai). When in prison, he worked to improve his Urdu and Tamizh.

Even though most of Gandhiji's life was spent speaking in English, he wrote his autobiography, *Satya Na Prayogo Athva Aatmakatha*, in his mother tongue, Gujarati. They appeared as 166 individual chapters in his own journal, *Navjivan*, between 1921 and 1929. They were also translated to Hindi and English. They were first published in 1948 as a single book, *An Autobiography or The Story of My Experiments with Truth*, in the US by the Public Affairs Press of Washington, DC.

Gandhiji was a strong proponent of Hindustani, a language that both, Hindus and Muslims in the country were comfortable with. He was totally against Sanskritization (adding more Sanskrit words to Hindustani) or Persianization (adding more Persian words to Hindustani) of the language.

In those days, there was a huge communication gap between the British rulers, the elite English-speaking Indians, and a vast majority of the Indian population that did not understand or speak English at all, which was the language of governance at the time. Gandhiji believed that a common language such as Hindustani, would help create a world that was inclusive and supported the needs of every individual, irrespective of their mother tongue, caste, creed, religion, cultural, and economic backgrounds.

He wanted freedom and rightful living for all minorities including the Parsis, Christians, and Sikhs. His final fast at the Birla House in Delhi, where he was assassinated, was to ensure that refugees on either side of the border were given justice and treated with respect. That there was harmony among the different communities living within a country as diverse as India. A language (Hindustani) that united the two was as important as anything else.

But little did he know that his support for Hindustani would be one of the reasons that led to his assassination.

Nathuram Godse, his assassin, was a firm believer in a country that was purely Hindu in every way. He did not believe in discrimination based on economic status, but he believed that the nation and its people should only practice Hinduism. That's why he started believing that Gandhiji was a proponent of Muslims.

In his final trial in court after he assassinated Gandhiji, Godse revealed that one of the reasons he shot the Mahatma was his patronage for Muslims through his love and support for Hindustani and Urdu! He hated the fact that Gandhiji championed Hindustani, which, according to him was a mere dialect, lacking grammar, or even a proper script! How could such a dialect become the official language of India? Godse thought it was simply preposterous to even consider such a thing. Hindi was the only way to go, according to him.

Gandhiji's dream, as we know, never came true and Hindi, a language that was primarily spoken only in the north of India, became one of our official languages.

Since then, Hindi has dominated the language landscape of our country and contributed to the endangerment and extinction of many other languages that made our country rich and diverse.

Tuti-e-Hind or the Parrot of India. The Voice of India. The Father of Urdu Literature. The Father of Qawwali (religious Islamic poetry and songs). These are some of the titles bestowed upon the most eminent Urdu poet of all times, Ab'ul Hassan Yamin ud-Din Khusrao, popularly known to the world as Hazrat Amir Khusrao Dehlavi.

Born in Uttar Pradesh, in the early thirteenth century, to a Turkic father and an Indian mother, Khusrao was a very intelligent child. He was proficient in Turkic, Persian and Arabic but his writings were in Hindustani because just like Gandhiji, he too believed that it was the language that united the whole of India.

Not only did he invent the sitar and the tabla, he popularized Hindustani or Hindavi in the royal courts during the Delhi Sultanate period with his mesmerizing poetry, riddles, word puzzles, and *dohas*, which mean couplets or two-line poetry.

A FRENCH RiVIERA iN INDIA

The Story of Puducherry's
Official Language

'Bonsoir!' say a bunch of passers-by. The bells chime
in a Gothic-styled church as the sun drizzles its last rays
on pastel-coloured buildings. Take a casual stroll down
Ville Blanche and the aroma of freshly baked croissants
invites you inside the butter-fragrant French patisseries
and cafés. The swaying palm trees by the boulevard along
the seaside is reminiscent of the French Riviera.

But this is not France we're talking about. This is
Pondicherry (now Puducherry), fondly known as Pondy.

The multilingual Union Territory (UT) of Puducherry,
a small enclave located on the Bay of Bengal along the
south-east coast of India, consists of the former French

colonies of Puducherry and Karaikal in Tamil Nadu, Mahe in Kerala, and Yanam in Andhra Pradesh.

Puducherry was a small fishing hamlet when the French came to India for trade in 1674. With the Portuguese, the Dutch, and the British setting up trading colonies and settlements in India, the French were not going to be left behind.

Under the rule of King Louis XIV, the French established their first trading ports in India—where goods were exchanged, imported, and exported, and factories were set up—in 1668 at Surat in Gujarat and in 1669 at Masulipatam (now Machilipatnam) in Andhra Pradesh. The French East India Company, or La Compagnie Française des Indes Orientales, set up their first township in Chandernagore, West Bengal, in 1673. This is where the first French nationals lived. They then headed south towards Puducherry.

They acquired Puducherry from the Sultan of Bijapur and set up a trading port there too. They chiefly bought cotton and silk textiles, and spices including the famous Malabar pepper.

The French did not stop there. They soon added Yanam (1723), Mahe (1725), and Karaikal (1739) to their territories; together they were known as Établissements français dans l'Inde (French Establishments in India).

Wars were fought along the Coromandel Coast. Puducherry came under temporary possession of the Dutch and the British, several times after the French lost the battles, but eventually it came back under French control.

In 1765, Puducherry became the capital of French India. The French were different compared to the other colonizers—while the British were busy looting the country of its values and valuables, the French built their territories while keeping the well-being of the Indians at the heart of their administration.

They continued to rule in their five dominions for nearly two centuries. However, their rule in India ended in 1954 and the French colonies became a part of India, when they were handed over to the newly formed Indian government, but on a condition.

The Indian government agreed to preserve the French history, culture, and tradition in Puducherry. One of the terms in the treaty they signed to agree upon it read: 'The French language shall remain the official language of the Establishments so long as the elected representatives of the people shall not decide otherwise.'

Puducherry had been declared a union territory and the French government gave the French citizens living there six months to decide if they wanted to retain their citizenship or give it up and become Indian citizens.

On the other hand, Indians were given a choice to obtain French citizenship and either stay in the union territory or move to France, while officially renouncing their original castes and traditions.

Many moved to France. Many continued to stay in India while keeping their French citizenship intact. These French-Pondicherrians are proud of their rich French heritage, something that sets them apart from the rest of the country.

The dominant language across the union territory is Tamizh due to its geographic location. While Tamizh continues to be the official language of the four enclaves, especially in Puducherry and Karaikal, the other official languages are Malayalam in Yanam, and Telugu in Mahe. French, English, and Hindi are also official languages.

There is a generation of people that prides in speaking French as a first language and the legacy of the French connection lives on with the people through various cultures and traditions. Wedding ceremonies are still conducted in both French and Tamizh and in many schools, French is offered as the first or second language and is also the medium of instruction. Both the governments are working hard to ensure that newer generations continue to learn about their Indo-French heritage. This is what makes Puducherry a major tourist attraction and it does everything from hosting French food festivals, to celebrating the Bastille Day (beginning of the French revolution) on 14 July each year with great pomp.

The French accent is not the only impact the French has had on the tongues of the French-Pondicherrians. It's also the French food that has tingled their tastebuds, giving birth to Puducherry's creole cuisine—fusion food that's a blend of two or more cultures, typically one European and one African or South Asian culture. In this case, it's French and south Indian. For instance, the popular French Bouillabaisse (fish stew) is Meen Puyabaise, where the stew is rich in Indian spices such as turmeric and tamarind but not as hot, just like the French would like it. Puducherry also enjoys the influence of Vietnamese, Cambodian, and Chinese cuisines because of the many Pondicherrians who were sent to fight wars in those countries.

While the French language thrives in the hamlets of Puducherry and the other former French colonies, there's one other colonial language in India that did not get the same support as French. It's the Portuguese creole. The Portuguese were the first Europeans to colonize

India. Wherever they went, language creoles or 'contact languages' were born. In and around the Bombay region, there was the Portuguese-Marathi creole, the Portuguese-Tamizh creole in the south-east and the Portuguese-Gujarati creole in Daman and Diu. William Rozario was the last speaker of the Portuguese-Malayalam creole of Cochin. Having said that, while Portuguese is not the official language of Goa anymore, Goa still has a few thousand proud Portuguese or Lusophone speakers, as they are known.

The French-speaking population of Puducherry is on the decline, what with an increasing number of French-Tamizh descendants moving to France for better job prospects and to reunite with their families who had opted to move to France.

The French colonization of India lasted for nearly three centuries, which means that generation after generation of people have been raised under a French cultural influence. A large part of the people from the French colonies spoke French as their mother tongue—they thought and ideated in French. There are some French-Pondicherrian authors who are writing in French and keeping French literature in India alive. But, sadly, readers for these books are few and far between.

The silver lining, however, is a section of the Puducherry population that's proud of their heritage and are fighting to keep it thriving whether it's through the restoration of French colonial buildings, the celebration of special French festivals and foods, or teaching the French language to newer generations. They believe that it's the heritage passed down to them from their ancestors and even though it became a part of their ancestral legacy through colonization, it's theirs now—an integral part of their identity.

JAMWA CHALO!

The Story of India's Refugee Languages

Picture this. An old and quintessentially Parsi house in the Dadar Parsi Colony in Mumbai, the single largest colony of Parsis living anywhere on this planet. It is redolent with the smells of a Parsi *bhonu* which is laid on a large dining table. '*Sufachat maidan*,' says an old Parsi uncle after polishing off his meal of chicken farcha, patra ni machhi and dhansak. This wonderful community with an uncanny sense of humour is as integral and important to the country as any other.

For centuries, people from different parts of the world have migrated all across the globe. Often, it's out of choice: to explore better education prospects, opportunities for economic prosperity, improved ways of living.

Sometimes, they move to avoid natural calamities like floods, draughts, tornadoes, earthquakes, and so on.

But there are times when people have no choice but to migrate: during wars or when countries are partitioned (for instance, when India split into India, Pakistan, and Bangladesh), or when they are forced to convert to a different religion. If they resist, they could be persecuted or even killed. And so, people migrate—across continents and oceans—to a place where they would be accepted and respected for who they are.

The Parsis were one such community of refugees who were seeking shelter in other countries and who are now settled primarily along the west coast of India in Gujarat and Maharashtra. They are the Zoroastrians who left Sassanid Iran or Persia in the seventh century to escape religious persecution by the Arab Muslims. Historically, Sassanid Iran was present-day Iran and Iraq put together. The Persians, as they were known, practised the religion of Zoroastrianism.

The Arabs invaded Persia after 635 CE (seventh century). Though the Zoroastrians put up a fight, they were never an aggressive community. Either due to coercion or for economic reasons, many Zoroastrians converted to Islam. And the ones who did not want to bow down, left.

Their arduous journey—by land, and across rough and stormy seas—led them to Diu on the west coast of

India. Iran had already established trade relations with India and hence they were aware of the routes and the trading ports.

Back then, the Zoroastrians spoke Persian, the native language of Persia. After spending nineteen years in Diu, they decided to move towards mainland India. They came to Sanjan in Gujarat, which was ruled by King Jadi (Jadhav) Rana.

Now, Jadi Rana was a kind king. He welcomed them and gave them asylum.

However, Jadi Rana laid down certain terms and conditions for them. They would never carry any weapons, their women would wear saris like the local women, their priests would explain Zoroastrianism to the king, and they would speak the local language—Gujarati.

Language was one of the chief concerns for the Zoroastrians. They preferred to use Persian because it was in Persian that all their religious ceremonies were conducted. It was in Persian they thought and prayed.

But no one in Gujarat knew Persian. How would such different ethnic groups communicate with each other? How would they connect, share, and live together?

The Parsis had no option but to yield. Time went by, and the Parsis put in a lot of effort to learn Gujarati. From speaking Persian with a spattering of Gujarati, over the years, they started speaking Gujarati with a sprinkling of Persian.

Did you know that the Zoroastrians who stayed back in Persia and migrated to India only later in the nineteenth century, continue to speak in Persian and are known as Iranis and not Parsis?

While the Parsis speak Gujarati, there is a certain distinctiveness to the way they speak it. Some call it Gujarati, some call it Parsi-Gujarati, a dialect of Gujarati, and some even call Parsi an independent language, which is soon losing itself to English. Newer generations of Parsis prefer to speak in the more dominant state languages of Hindi, Gujarati, and English rather than their mother tongue.

Even though the Parsis had a very different accent compared to the local Gujaratis, they blended seamlessly along the west coast of India. Whether they were in Bombay in Maharashtra, or Sanjan, Udwada, Surat, and Navsari in Gujarat, they started speaking the local language of Gujarati or Marathi while staying true to their culture and heritage, thus maintaining their unique identity. If someone calls out, *jamwa chalo*, which means 'come, let's eat' in Gujarati, you will not be able to tell whether the person is a Gujarati or a Parsi unless it's followed by *bhonu taiyar chhe* or 'meal is ready', where *bhonu* is a typical Parsi word for 'meal'.

It's interesting to note that while all countries that the Arab Muslims invaded, converted to Islam, and adopted their culture and language, only Iran did not. The Persians were the only people who protected and preserved their traditions and their language. They even created their own sect of Islam known as Shiaism. After the Mughal invasion of Iran, the Zoroastrians who remained in Iran encouraged the Mughals to speak in Persian, and when the Mughals came to India, they made Parsi their court language too!

If you visit the Red Fort or Lal Quila in Delhi, you can read these Persian words engraved in gold on its walls:

Agar firdaus bar ru-ye zamin ast
Hamin ast-o hamin ast-o hamin ast
This means:
'If there is heaven on earth,
it is this, it is this, it is this.'

The Parsis have strict rules of defining who a Parsi is, and those orthodox rules have contributed to a decline in their population and in turn the number of people speaking their language. Their population is around 60,000 across India (according to the 2011 census) out of which approximately 40,000 to 45,000 speak Parsi. According to Article 341 and 342 of the Indian Constitution, if their population goes under 30,000, they will be termed as a 'tribe', not even a community.

But there are passionate Parsis who are working to protect and preserve their culture and heritage. Meher Marfatia and Sooni Taraporewala are two such people. They are Parsi language activists and the authors of *Parsi Bol,* a compilation of hilarious, tongue-in-cheek Parsi idioms and phrases, with contributions from Parsis around the world.

Parsis were not the only refugees who began speaking Gujarati. There was another community that migrated to India in the eleventh and twelfth centuries from Egypt and Yemen—the Dawoodi Bohra community. They speak Lisan ud-Dawat, a language that has adopted vocabulary and other elements from Arabic, Persian, Urdu, as well as Gujarati.

The Dawoodi Bohras are Shia Muslims who migrated from Egypt and Yemen to western India and Pakistan, East Africa, and the Middle East. Since they first lived and traded in Gujarat, their mother tongue, Lisan al-Dawat, borrows heavily from Gujarati and has a Gujarati base, especially in syntax and grammar, while maintaining a flavour of Arabic and Persian. Even though most of them speak a version of Gujarati, their business backgrounds enable them to speak the language of the place they call home. For instance, nearly ten thousand Bohras live in Chennai and even though they speak in Lisan al-Dawat, they have welcomed the local culture and traditions and have learned to speak Tamizh as well.

The 2.5 million strong Sindhi speakers in India are also a refugee community. Ancient Sindh goes back to nearly 2400 years since the time of the Indus Valley Civilization and was a settlement around the Sindhu or the Indus River. Due to its geographic location, it was the target of many invasions—Arabs, Greeks, Turks, even the Mughals. These invasions caused the Sindhi language to be heavily influenced by other languages such as Arabic, Persian, Hindi, Turkish, and later, even English and Portuguese.

Post-Partition, while the Muslim Sindhi speakers stayed in Pakistan, the Hindu Sindhi speakers fled to India. This was a very turbulent time for the Sindhis who came back, because they were now people without a land, refugees in their own country. They settled in areas closest to the Sindh province, which is Kutchh in Gujarat and Maharashtra. The Sindhi speakers in Pakistan had to blend with the Urdu and Persian speakers, whereas those in India started to speak Sindhi with an influence of Hindi, Gujarati, and Marathi. Soon, Sindhi grew and adapted into many avatars or dialects—Vichori, Lari, Lasi, Siroli, Kutchhi, Thari, among others. A language as ancient as Sindhi is now spoken in many parts of the world in various dialects, all surviving in one way or another.

Be it Parsis or Bohras or Sindhis, their unique languages define their strong identities. Just like these languages, there are thousands of other languages that have evolved over time, adapting to different conditions such as political issues, migration of people, invasions, and more. These communities, who initially arrived in our country as refugees, are now one of us.

ALL ABOUT ENGLISH-VINGLISH

The Story of English in India

'Become Fluent in English.'

'Best Online English Course.'

'Learn English in Just Ten Days!'

These are some of the innumerable ads for online and offline courses that offer to teach spoken and written English in India. They are popular in both urban and rural regions. Everyone aspires to have a better life with better-paying jobs and whether one likes it or not, these jobs require people to know English.

Western countries have colonized India since the fifteenth century, beginning with the Portuguese in 1498, followed by the Dutch, the French, and lastly, the

British. While all colonizing countries left something behind, one of the things that the British left behind was their language—English.

English is one of our twenty-two official languages. It all began with an act that designated English as an official language and a medium of instruction in schools. Thomas Babington Macaulay is a name to reckon with when it comes to English education in India. He was sent to India in 1834 to do what the East India Company could not.

Macaulay was a shrewd historian and politician who was proud of his language and boasted of how intellectually superior it was to languages such as Sanskrit, Urdu, or Persian in every way. According to him, Sanskrit and Urdu were languages in which only religious texts were written. If the Indians needed a progressive education, it had to be in English.

However, before English entered India's education system, things were quite different. Earlier, there were two types of institutions in India—those that taught in Sanskrit and those that taught in Urdu.

The British maintained that while Sanskrit and Arabic were languages rich in poetry and works of fiction, it was English and the other European languages that reigned supreme in matters of science and other factual subjects. They advocated that only English would help people pursue higher studies—whether in India or abroad.

It would give them access to better jobs and improve their quality of life. Indians also started demanding an education where the language of instruction was English because, according to them, that was the only sure and fast way of moving up the ladder in society.

And just like that, the use of English spread across the country like a forest fire that was hard to curb. The Charter Act passed in 1813 made the East India Company responsible for making education compulsory for all Indians. It was much easier for the rest of the country to learn one language than the British to learn so many. They wanted to raise a generation of 'English natives' who spoke like the British and, therefore, showed less resistance towards them—a class of people known as the Anglicists, who spoke their language in the same way the British did and acted as interpreters to the millions of people whom they had been governing. These Anglicists would soon outnumber the Orientalists, who believed that Indians should stay true to their roots and culture by studying only in regional and mother tongues. They would now serve as English-speaking Indian servants in the British government—skilled yet cheap labour.

At the time Macaulay came to India, Persian was the official language of the government of India. But Macaulay's 'Minute' on education changed everything.

Lord William Bentinck, then governor general of India, took up Macaulay's 'Minute' and on 2 February 1835, he passed the English Education Act of 1835, which made English an official medium of instruction. All government funds that were formerly used for teaching Sanskrit and Persian were now directed towards teaching literature and sciences in English alone. English became the primary or first language, whereas the regional languages now received secondary status.

Slowly yet steadily, universities that taught English as a first language were established in Calcutta (Kolkata), Bombay (Mumbai), and Madras (Chennai) in 1857. It started replacing Persian as an official language for all administrative purposes and was the language of communication between the elite class and the press.

Post-Independence, the Constitution of India was written in English, even before it was declared an official language of India. Our then prime minister, Jawaharlal Nehru, was stuck in a challenging situation. He had to play his cards right because the Indians were in a very fragile state after the partition of the country into East Pakistan (Bangladesh) and West Pakistan (Pakistan). Annexation of states on linguistic lines also added to his complications. How could he make English an official language when his own people were fighting for their identities, for their cultures to be acknowledged? At the same time, how could he do away with English, which had become such an integral part of India's education system?

In 1950, it was decided that English would continue to be used for official purposes in the government of

India for the next fifteen years, after which it would be discontinued. But with more and more people seeking education in English, it was going to be impossible and perhaps even foolish to completely abolish English from the list of India's official languages.

After much consideration, Nehru devised the three-language formula, whereby, each Hindi-speaking state would use Hindi, English, and the dominant regional language for official purposes and the non-Hindi-speaking states would include their regional language, Hindi, and English, in that order. In the Official Languages Act of 1963, it was decided that English would be used as a co-official language alongside Hindi in the Hindi-speaking states, whereas it would be an official language in states that had not adopted Hindi as their official language.

English became an official language of communication within the Parliament too, but it wasn't easy. There was opposition from both sides for the three-language formula.

'Why not *only* Hindi?' questioned the Hindi-speaking states of northern India.

'Why *only* Hindi?' questioned the non-Hindi-speaking states of south India.

Tamil Nadu declared the day the act was passed as a day of mourning for Tamilians. Their problem was not that Hindi was being taught in their state—the problem was that it was being *forcefully* taught. They have always maintained that people of any state must have the right to learn any language they wish to—they should not be made to learn a language that doesn't make sense to them. They were clearly anti-imposition, not anti-language. The Tamilians have always been proud of their mother tongue and fought hard to protect and preserve it. Even today, Tamil Nadu has the least number of Hindi speakers in all of India. They stuck to their guns and followed the two-language formula (Tamizh-English), instead of the three-language formula (Tamizh-Hindi-English).

Did you know that Thanith Tamil Iyakkam or the Independent Tamil Movement, started in 1916, was a language purity movement whereby Tamil scholars put in tireless efforts to weed out borrowed words and loan words from other languages and make Tamil or Tamizh a pure language?

Gandhiji was proficient in English. He wrote and spoke in excellent and powerful English and the British acknowledged it. But he still opposed an entire education system that glorified English in a way that downplayed our mother languages. Rabindranath Tagore, though he wrote in Bengali, translated his own works to English as well.

It is Sir Raja Ram Mohan Roy who is one of the pioneers of Indian literature in English. He was an independent journalist who wrote and published many essays that highlighted the plight of women in the country. He translated many important texts such as the *Upanishads* and the *Vedanta* in English. He emphasized on the importance of studying science, technology, Western medicine, and English to Indians.

We may or may not speak English fluently, but if we eat, dress, work, and live like them, we are as English as the English themselves. We have reached a stage where English has become a very integral part of our lives— at school, at work, at home, and it even allows us to go global in education and trade.

It's interesting to note that there are local versions of English in India where English heavily borrows vocabulary from the local Indian languages. Some of them are Hinglish (Hindi and English), Kanglish (Kannada and English), Tenglish (Telugu and English). They are known as 'portmanteaus' or words that combine the sounds and meanings of two different words. Those who speak in these hybrid languages frequently interchange between the two said languages while speaking.

While India tops the list of English-speaking countries in the world as a primary language (as of 2021), we must remember that the figure still represents only around 10 per cent of our vast population. Many other languages have been lost to English forever.

The cursive system of writing, where letters or even symbols are looped together to flow as one, exists primarily to increase our speed of writing and, sometimes, for a more aesthetic appeal. There are many examples of cursive systems of writing the world over: from the ancient Egyptians, who had the hieratic and demotic scripts in addition to the hieroglyphics, which was a painstaking and time-consuming way of writing in daily life; the Greeks, who have been using a cursive variant of their script since the ninth century; the Russians, whose cursive writing looks similar to the English cursive; and the Chinese, who have something known as a 'rough script' that simplifies their highly complex logographic system of writing.

Once upon a time, the Marathi language, written in the Devanagari script, also had a cursive script of its own. Known as the Modi script, it originated in the 1400s as a cursive way of speed-writing Marathi literature. 'Modi' is derived from the Marathi word *modne*, which means to 'bend' or 'break'. This script quite literally bent and broke the Devanagari letters in a way that helped people write Marathi much faster. The Marathas encouraged the use of the Modi script and it was used extensively in literati circles.

But the wiggly, round letters of the Modi script were tough to typeset and print on paper as compared to the much cleaner Devanagari script. Moreover, post-Independence, the ideology that each language must be written in one and only one script did not spare Marathi and it was evident that Marathi would be continued to be written either in Devanagari or in Modi. All doubts were laid to rest when Maharashtra was created on linguistic lines and Devanagari was declared as the official script for Marathi.

The Modi script gradually faded with time. No one wrote in the script that was used to write some of the finest Marathi literature, among many other important documents, again.

Just like the Modi script, there are many languages and scripts in India that are dead. There are many factors that drive languages to endangerment and extinction—apathy towards the speakers, invasion by other kingdoms and rulers, and migration, among others. Despite courageous efforts from impassioned language activists, it's been a tough journey to revitalize them. The stories in this section give you a glimpse of some important languages and scripts as they moved along on their journey towards extinction.

TAATUNG TATUNG

The Story behind the World's Oldest Indigenous Language

She longed to speak to someone. It had been nearly four decades since she had spoken to anyone who knew her language. So, she spoke to the birds and sang songs to the trees.

> *er chuuo*
> *taatung tatung taatung tatung*
> *er chuuo*
> *taatung tatung taatung tatung*
> (Clean, clean the place,
> Dance, dance, dance, dance!
> Clean, clean the place,
> Dance, dance, dance, dance!)
> —*A Bo Song* sung by Boa Sr (F 80); Audio 7, Video 9
> *Voices from the Lost Horizon: Stories and Songs of the*
> *Great Andamanese* by Anvita Abbi

Perhaps, the chirping of the birds meant they understood her words. Perhaps, the swaying of the branches meant they understood her language. She would giggle and burst into laughter as she sang.

But these giggles and laughter ceased to exist one day. These songs, and her voice, are now forever silent.

Elder Boa Sr breathed her last on 26 January 2010 and with her, her language, race, and culture breathed their last too. Elder Boa Sr was the only remaining speaker of Aka-Bo, one of the indigenous languages of the archipelago of the Andaman and Nicobar Islands (ANI). This language dates to the pre-Neolithic (10,000–4500 BCE) era, and belongs to one of the oldest indigenous groups of this world who had first migrated out of Africa 70,000 years ago.

ANI is a tightly knit group of almost 324 islands to the south-east of the Indian subcontinent, giving an impression of being one big island. The Andaman Islands comprise the Great Andaman Islands, which include Great Andaman, Little Andaman, and the North Sentinel Islands. Four indigenous tribes inhabit these islands: the Jarawas, the Onges, the Great Andamanese, and the Sentinalese. These hunters and gatherers were the very first settlers of Southeast Asia. While their languages have the same ancestry, the Jarawas, the Onges, and the Sentinalese languages are different from Great Andamanese.

Great Andamanese is a group of ten languages spoken by ten different tribes who live in the north, the middle, and the south of the Great Andaman Islands. While the languages are distinct, they are quite similar too. Present-day Great Andamanese or PGA is a group of Jeru, Khora, Bo, and Sare languages. Unfortunately, we have lost the last speakers of Khora, Bo, and Sare, hence these languages are being driven to extinction. All that remains of the PGA or the Jeru now are about fifty-six people, with only seven speakers who know the language, that too not fluently. They are 'rememberers' of the language, more than speakers, that is, they speak the language only if they are asked to recall certain words in their language or use it as a secret code to speak around those who don't know the language. Most other times, they communicate in Andamanese Hindi.

But how did these tribes, who were hunters and gatherers and spoke languages that were endemic to the Andamans, start speaking in Hindi and other popular Indian languages?

These Andamanese tribes had been living on these islands in complete isolation from the rest of the world until the mid-nineteenth century, when the British forced them to leave their forests, their very homes.

The year 1857 was an important year in Indian history. It was just the beginning of our first war for independence from the British. After much consideration and deliberation, the British chose the Andamans, roughly 1255 km by sea from Kolkata, to send our freedom fighters or war prisoners for lifetime imprisonment. While what happened to the prisoners was much worse than just life imprisonment, this marked the beginning of a new era of settlements in the islands, the beginning of new cultures, traditions, and linguistic diversities.

But these new civilizations marked the end of an entire race of people who called the islands their home. The British did everything in their capacity to uproot the tribes. They built 'homes' where they captured young Andamanese children away from their families and forests. They got them used to an English and a more 'civilized' way of living. Their forests were destroyed to build colonies for prisoners. While most of the children ran back into the forests, many could not survive because they were neither here nor there—they couldn't go back to the forest or adapt themselves to a new lifestyle. Some were forced to become British servants.

Soon, the Andamans became an important holding area for freedom fighters. Within months, the number of inmates arriving at Port Blair increased from 200 to over 700, coming from across the country.

Many inmates died of starvation on the island. Many were killed while trying to escape. Many others were killed by the Andamanese, who were enraged at losing their forests, their only homes. However, this did not deter the British from sending more people to ANI, causing more damage to this untouched, rich, and biodiverse group of islands.

Although many inmates were sent back to their states on grounds of good conduct, many decided to settle on the islands. Several inmates married each other and started families. Colonies began to burgeon in and around Port Blair, with the Bengali settlers leading the way.

India's partition into Pakistan and Bangladesh also contributed to migration across the Bay of Bengal to ANI. With the Partition, while there was an exodus of Muslims out of India into Pakistan, there was an influx of Hindu refugees from Bangladesh into India. Bengal became the smallest yet most populated state in India and something had to be done to manage the population crisis. As a result, thousands of families from Bengal moved to the Andamans. They cleared forests, built houses, and cultivated food. From around 2300 Bengalis in 1951, their population rose to around 65,000 by 1991!

The population of the settlers kept increasing while those of the natives kept declining. In the 1970s, the construction of the nearly 330 km long Andaman Grand Trunk Road that runs across the length of the islands, connecting 400 islands between North Andaman and South Andaman and stretching from Port Blair in the north to Diglipur in the south, threatened the survival of the Great Andamanese and the Jarawas. While there is a law to protect the Jarawas from outsiders, the tourists made a mockery of the tribes—they introduced deadly diseases like measles against which these tribes had no immunity, stole their food and mistreated them.

The Great Andamanese were moved to the tiny Strait Island and sadly they are now a tribe dependent on the Indian government for food, shelter, and other basic necessities like clothing and medicine. Elder Boa Sr lamented the fact that while the Jarawas were fortunate to continue living in the forests, the Andamanese lost the art of hunting and gathering—something that defined their race—and their children know nothing about their cultures and traditions.

While Hindi (the Andamanese speak a dialect of Hindi) and English are the official languages of ANI, Bengali is the most spoken language in the Andamans with over a quarter of the population being Bangla-speaking people. Tamizh, Telugu, and Malayalam are the other spoken languages. The settlers were free in the island, but they also felt confined. The only way to survive on a remote island, was by practising their cultures and traditions, speaking their mother languages, and building communities.

The vulnerable tribal groups—the Andamanese, the Nicobarese, the Onges, the Jarawas, the Shompens—mainly speak Andamanese and Ongan languages. But there is one language in ANI that we know nothing about.

The Sentinalese people are the world's only uncontacted indigenous people—people who have never wished to establish contact with the rest of the world, let alone locals of ANI.

The Sentinalese live on the densely forested North Sentinel Island of ANI. An aura of mystery always surrounds them. Especially around how they communicate with each other. What language do they speak? Since making any sort of contact with them is a distant reality, linguists have tried to analyse their language based on their location with respect to the rest of the islands in the archipelago. Perhaps their language is similar to the languages of the Onge and Jarawa tribes who inhabit the Andamans, which is closest to the North Sentinel Island. Perhaps it would be easier to find out if their genetics and family origins could be traced.

But trying too hard to get to know this tribe better would only cause them harm. It could expose them to diseases they have never known and potentially endanger the existence of these 50–100 people who are content living in isolation. It would be best to respect their privacy and their right to live the way they wish to.

Conversations, stories, and songs are important influences when it comes to learning languages. They keep our languages alive. When we stop narrating stories to the next generation, stop singing songs and humming lullabies to babies, the language is on its path to extinction and the survival of the language rests on the shoulders of the handful of remaining speakers.

Sadly, this has happened to the fifty-six surviving Jerus or the PGA group. And it's been a challenge to keep Jeru alive. The only silver lining is that of their fifty-six surviving people, there are about twenty children who are young and who still have the opportunity to learn the language from their elders and the seven surviving speakers of the language.

Padma Shri Prof. Anvita Abbi, a tenacious linguist and scholar of South Asia's tribal and minority languages, and her team, have been trying to ensure that the oldest languages spoken on this planet do not vanish without being recorded. She has identified the sixth language family of India—Great Andamanese—and believes that Onge, Jarawa, and possibly Sentinelese may constitute a separate seventh language family. Along the way, she has recorded some of the oldest indigenous stories recounted by one of the speakers, Nao Sr, and songs of the very last speaker, Elder Boa Sr.

Prof. Abbi believes that while with the passage of time, the art of narrating a story may be lost, the singing of the songs is something that does not change. According to her, the lifespan of songs is longer than the language itself. She has created a brilliant dictionary of words, phrases, songs, and stories in the

Andamanese languages in the hope that speakers of the Andamanese languages increase and have someone else to speak with in these languages.

In this circle of life and death of these languages, there's much more at stake with the loss of each language than just words and sounds. We need more Anvita Abbis. Languages need the space to not just exist but to flourish, especially those that marked the beginning of communication for the human race.

μ

VANISHING VOICES OF THE SEVEN SISTERS

The Story of the Once Language-rich Northeast India

The Brahmaputra River is majestic—it is, after all, one of the longest rivers in the world. It flows from Tibet into India through Arunachal Pradesh, Assam, and culminates into the Bay of Bengal through Bangladesh. While the river brings with it rich and fertile alluvial soil, as well as floods and devastation, it also brought with it a language, hundreds of years ago.

In the thirteenth century, the river witnessed a mass exodus of the Tai people from Tibet to India. Most historians believe that the Tai community originally inhabited the Yunnan province of China, others believe they came from Burma, but whatever their true origin was, they had an identity of their own. Their cultures and traditions were uniquely Tai. However, over time, as various dynasties tried to capture their provinces, the Tai people felt the need to have their own kingdom. Thus began their search for a new region they could call the Tai-Ahom Kingdom.

King Chaolong Sukapha of the Tai people left China after a row with his older brother over who would ascend the throne. Along with nearly 9000 followers, he followed an ancient trade route between China and India, crossing the Patkai mountains, across the Brahmaputra River, that led him to the north of Assam. He never entered the Brahmaputra Valley as a conqueror. He befriended the local tribes, helped them in their agricultural pursuits, learned their languages, adopted their customs and traditions, and was accepted as one of them. After moving along the Brahmaputra Valley, looking for the best regions to cultivate rice, he finally took over as the local king without fighting a single battle.

Sukhapa established the Tai-Ahom kingdom in 1228 CE in the upper reaches of the Brahmaputra Valley. Charaideo became the kingdom's first capital in 1261. This kingdom was undefeatable for 600 glorious years (till 1828), much like its name, Ahom, which means 'invincible'.

Did you know that the name Assam is derived from 'asama' in Ahom, which means 'invincible' too?

Tai-Ahom was the only language spoken in Assam for those 600 years. It was a direct descendent of the Proto-Tai group of languages. But, suddenly, a day arrived when no one spoke Tai-Ahom. The only traces of the language were the religious scriptures and the Ahomiya rituals performed by the priests.

What happened? How did the speakers of a language suddenly vanish?

While Tai-Ahom prospered in the Brahmaputra Valley, there was an Indo-Aryan language that made its way into Assam. It was the Assamese or the Asamiya language. Asamiya was born from Magadhi, from which were also born Bengali, Oriya and Maithili. Over time, Asamiya entered the Ahom court and then made its way into the Ahomiya households. And soon enough, Asamiya replaced Ahom.

It was Francis Buchana-Hamilton, a Scottish physician and surveyor in the East India Company who first recorded that Ahom was a dead language in 1808-09, in his survey of eastern India. He learned that even the Ahom priests, who knew the language and could study its script, had forgotten how the language sounded.

The Ahoms stayed but their language ceased to exist. The wisdom that the language brought with it ceased to exist. Only stories from the Ahom kingdom, known as Buranjis, written in the Ahom language, remain.

Ahom, the westernmost of the Tai language family, gave in to Asamiya due to a multitude of reasons: Asamiya cultural dominance, job opportunities in more popular languages, invasions from Burma, and battles that weakened the Ahom kingdom. The last straw was when it was annexed by the British East India Company after signing the Treaty of Yandabo.

Linguists are still perplexed: how could a language so complete as Ahom, and used for 600 years, disappear completely? However, Ahom is not the only language that's extinct. Tai-Turung, another Tai language that was spoken in Assam is now extinct—their population also speaks primarily in Assamese now. There are many other languages in Northeast India that are endangered or moribund. Some languages have only very senior speakers, which means that if the language is not learned by the next generation, it will easily go extinct in less than two to three decades.

A moribund language is a critically endangered language that is almost about to go extinct because no children are likely to speak it as their first language. For instance, the Nihali or Nahali language with only about 2000–2500 speakers known as Nihals, in Central India (Maharashtra and Madhya Pradesh) is a critically endangered pre-Indo-Aryan, pre-Dravidian, and pre-Munda language. In fact, most linguists have concluded that the Nihal language does not belong to any of the known language families. Most Nihals now prefer to speak in Marathi or Hindi for better socio-economic prospects.

Northeast India is one of the most linguistically diverse regions in the world. There are more than an estimated 220 languages spoken by nearly fifty-six million people living in the seven sister states of Arunachal Pradesh, Assam, Manipur, Meghalaya, Mizoram, Nagaland and Tripura and the brother state of Sikkim (it does not share a border with the other seven states).

While they do share borders, they neither share the same languages nor the same language families. Indo-European, Sino-Tibetan, Tai, Austro-Asiatic, and other creole language families all co-exist in this region. To add to its woes, Northeast India is fast converting to Christianity, making English the primary language of many, which is a further deterrent to preserving mother languages. While English is the dominant language of many tribes and indigenous communities, Hindi is also not too far behind. In fact, while Arunachal Pradesh enjoys over fifty distinct languages, Hindi is its most spoken language.

It's a known fact that only those languages with scripts of their own are considered as 'proper languages'. The rest are passed off as dialects or other forms of a language that do not qualify them as official or state languages. There are dedicated individuals and organizations who are working towards the revitalization of these vanishing voices of the Northeast.

For instance, Palash Kumar Nath, a linguist from Assam, is trying to preserve the Tai-Khamyang language that has only a handful of speakers between the ages of seventy and eighty years.

From mapping the language in the Singhpo script to starting the Singhpo Mother Tongue School in the Ketetong village, he introduced Tai-Khamyang to children through storybooks, dictionaries, and other language learning books. Sadly, the school shut down due to lack of funding and any administrative support.

While groups of individuals are being trained in each Northeastern language to prevent them from going extinct, measures are also being taken to revive languages such as Ahom, even though it would never be possible to recreate the language the way it was spoken or written earlier. If these measures are not taken and if the right policies for the preservation of endangered languages are not enforced, the death of not just languages, but entire cultures and populations is imminent.

But is this enough to keep our languages from perishing?

3

'TEN THOUSAND DOLLARS, ANYONE?'

The Story of the World's Only Undeciphered Language

The air around the farmhouse near the district of Hisar in Haryana was hot and arid. A team of about twenty-five students and ten faculty members led by Dr Vasant Shinde from the Archaeological Department of Deccan College in Pune, and a forensic team from Seoul National University, South Korea, sat, starry-eyed, around a wealth of antique artefacts—inscribed seals and pot sherds, precious ornaments, toys, seals, and skeletons of a few bodies, among other things. And this is just after excavating two of the seven mounds at the site they were working on, in a nondescript village known as Rakhigarhi. While these excavations had happened between 2011–2016, they had just time-travelled to about 5500 BCE to uncover what would be the bedrock of an entire civilization housed under dust and soil.

This nondescript village they were near was precisely where one of the largest Harappan Civilization sites had been discovered at 350 hectares, surpassing the famous Mohenjo-Daro site. The Rakhigarhi site, which was first discovered by archaeologist Amarendra Nath of ASI from 1998–2000, was now front and centre on the heritage world map as one of the largest and most significant archaeological sites: The Harappan or Indus Valley Civilization or IVC.

IVC was an urban civilization that burgeoned on the banks of the Indus-Saraswati river basins. It was a civilization of ginormous proportions, meticulous planning, precise constructions, architectural marvels, significant cultures, with an estimated 50,000 people possessing extraordinary intellectual capabilities inhabiting it.

Until one fine day, every trace of this civilization that had flourished between 2600 BCE and 1900 BCE disappeared. For 4000 years, this civilization remained hidden from the world until the nineteenth century when some labourers, who were laying a 100-mile-long railway track between Lahore and Karachi (modern-day Pakistan) in British India, accidentally discovered the first fire-baked brick from one of the walls of this enormous township. The labourers used the nearly uniform bricks to lay the road, unaware of the fact that the bricks belonged to one of the oldest civilizations of this world.

How did this civilization, also referred to as Meluhha or 'the high country' (because of the height it was built at) in the Mesopotamian texts, simply vanish?

Did the people go extinct, did other civilizations invade it, did they succumb to diseases and epidemics, or did they migrate to different civilizations in response to sudden climatic changes, such as the drying up of the Saraswati river that was a chief natural resource for many of their cities, or did natural calamities force them to abandon their homes? A theory that the Aryans either invaded the civilization or migrated to their cities and merged with them is also something that has been considered. While we already know so much about the life and times of this civilization, there are still so many mysteries that surround it.

These planned townships are still being actively excavated 100 years after they were first discovered by noted archaeologist Rai Bahadur Daya Ram Sahni of the Archaeological Survey of India (ASI) in Harappa, Punjab (now Pakistan) in 1921. Many epigraphists, linguists, and archaeologists have studied more than 3500 short inscriptions made on ceramic, clay, terracotta, bronze, and copper seals and tablets discovered at the many Harappan sites. These 1-inch by 1-inch square and sometimes round, stamped, and carved seals have animals such as bulls, bison, rhinos, tigers, elephants, fish, and human figures, with a series of signs and symbols to go with them. These seals have been found even as far as the Mesopotamian civilization, indicating that the Harappans had well-established trade relations as far as present-day Middle East. The seals were tied to bales of goods that were sent across long distances from the banks of the Indus to Mesopotamia—the integrity of the seals guaranteed that the goods were not tinkered with.

All these signs and symbols must mean something—the driving factor behind the commendable attempts and plausible theories that have been proposed to decipher the script and language hidden within this enigmatic pictographic script, has posed more questions than given answers. Some experts have even suggested that the pictures and motifs on the seals convey the phonetic sound of the text for those who do not know how to read, also known as the rebus technique. For instance, if the text is 'belief', the motif could be that of a 'bee' and a 'leaf'. Some have proposed that they are just non-linguistic symbols, not a proper written language with syntax and grammar. There are others who have compared the script to other ancient scripts like Brahmi, Sumerian, Egyptian, Mesopotamian, again without much success.

There are many reasons that underline these unsuccessful attempts. Some epigraphists argue that the script can be deciphered the way Greek was—through identification of roots and suffixes, guessing the pronunciation of certain syllables and symbols, and so on.

But the discovered inscriptions are too short to make any sense, making this approach almost impossible. With an average length of only five symbols stringed together to the longest ones being twenty-six symbols, that too, only in two texts found till date, it's difficult for epigraphists to understand phonetics, repetition, and other clues that can help them decode the text. While some civilizations had artefacts with inscriptions appearing in more than one language, making identification easier, Harappa didn't. No epics or religious texts, which could give an idea of the language they spoke, have been found either.

A civilization spread over a million square km may have had people who spoke one language, but with variation in dialects across geographies.

Epigraphist Padma Shri Iravatham Mahadevan dedicated most of his life in deciphering the Indus script. He made a strong case to prove that the script was an early form of the Dravidian (south Indian, such as Tamizh, Telugu, and Kannada) script. He presented his theory by comparing Indus signs and sequences that appeared frequently with the Dravidian script. Through computer analysis, he also proved that the Indus language had only suffixes, like the Dravidian languages, and no prefixes, like the Indo-Aryan languages.

Mahadevan also contested that the mysterious language called Brahui, a Dravidian language that is still spoken by a community of people in faraway Pakistan, can be strong evidence that the Dravidian languages were spoken in the Indus civilizations of Harappa and Mohenjo-Daro.

Brahui is the name of a two-million strong tribe living in the Balochistan province of Pakistan who speak a language by the same name—Brahui. It is written in the Arabic and Latin scripts, not Brahmi. Over time, the language has been heavily influenced by the dominant Indo-Aryan languages of the region such as Baloch, Urdu, Sindhi, and Persian but the language continues to be inherently Dravidian.

Whatever be the language or the script, one thing that the academicians and researchers are quite certain about is that majority of the writing is from right to left. In many inscriptions, while the symbols starting from right were equidistant, they seemed to be cramped up towards the left, indicating that the owner of that inscription realized only later that they did not have enough space to finish writing the text.

The signboard at the entrance of the citadel at the Dholavira site in Kutch is the biggest existing inscription to have been discovered till date. It is 3 metres in length and has one symbol that repeats itself four times. Some say it is a signboard that fell on its face and left impressions in the stone, some say it is the inscription on a tombstone and if the stone underneath was excavated, one would most likely find skeletons of the buried.

As more and more similar artefacts are being discovered at disparate sites in the Indian subcontinent, it is becoming increasingly evident that the Harappan Civilization was larger and older than we think or know. There are nearly 2000 archaeological sites, of which over 850 sites are in India—the rest of the sites went to Pakistan after our country was partitioned in 1947.

It's been over a century and Indologists are still trying to crack this puzzle of grand proportions. This is a language that may have gone extinct or merged with other languages as the people started migrating and blending with other civilizations, existing in an avatar that no one knows. Or perhaps, we may even be speaking this language without knowing its ancestral tapestry.

In 2004, an anonymous donor offered a reward of USD 10,000 to anyone who could crack this mysterious script from Meluhha, but it still lies unclaimed. One can only hope that we shall eventually be able to tell whether this mysterious language perished completely, or whether it continues to live on the tongues of many around the world.

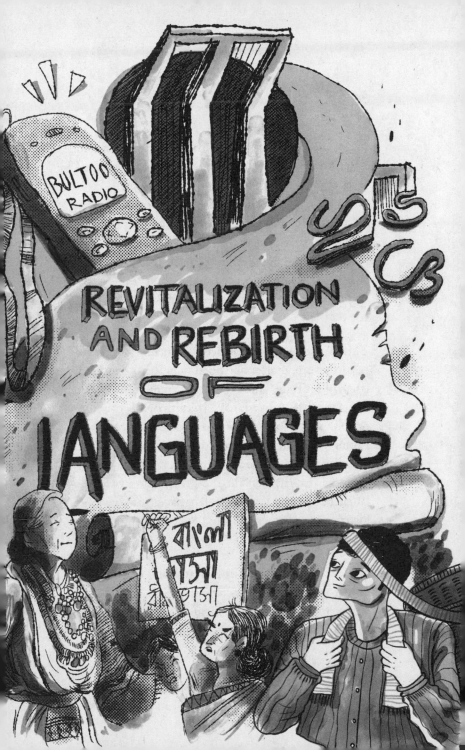

He's a man on a mission. And not just any mission. After documenting 780 languages in India (around seventy to eighty languages were out of reach), Prof. Ganesh Devy is documenting over 6000 languages across the world. He believes that conserving languages will conserve the human race. In India, 70 per cent of the population speak 30 per cent of the languages, whereas 30 per cent of the people speak 70 per cent of the languages—and this man wants to correct that.

This thinker, linguist and activist's main objective is to conserve, revitalize, and document the endangered languages of the more than 104 million Adivasis living in India. Adivasis have a wealth of information on our vast biodiversity and indigenous cultures. Losing their languages would mean losing all their knowledge too. There are many initiatives that Prof. Devy has undertaken for the preservation of these languages because if these languages survive, the identity of these endangered speech communities also survives.

One of them is the Bhasha Research and Publication Centre at Baroda (1996), which has collaborated with other research institutes and volunteers who help him to reach out to tribals so the many unknown, vulnerable and endangered languages can be documented and published. One of the most fascinating things that the centre does is publish a magazine, *Dhol*, in eleven tribal languages—Ahirani, Bhantu, Bhil, Choudhary, Dehwali, Dungri Bhili, Garasiya, Gor-Banjara, Kunkana, Panchmahali Bhili, Pavri, Rathwi—where the tribals take charge and share their cultural knowledge with each other through the magazine.

Language reformists like Prof. Devy understand that every language is a living entity and that each one of them goes through its own life-cycle—from having known or unknown ancestor origins, to adapting to changing circumstances, to either flourishing or then disappearing. Where one language dies, another language is born somewhere, and this saga of birth, death, and rebirth of languages will continue so long as the human race survives.

The stories in this section give us hope that all is not lost yet. That if sincere efforts are made to revitalize languages, they will live on to share their stories with the world for generations to come.

1

EKUSHEY

The Story of World Mother Language Day

The Bangla (or Bengali) Language Movement, which started on *Ekushey* (twenty-first in Bangla) February, was a significant day, not only in the history of Bangladesh but in the history of this world. This language movement began with the end of British rule in India.

India's independence from the tyrannical British Raj on 15 August 1947, which lasted for two centuries, was without a doubt one of the best things that could have happened to our country at the time. But this freedom came at a huge price. It fractured a country based on religious beliefs.

India was divided into the Union of India (with a Hindu majority) and Pakistan (with a Muslim majority). Pakistan had two parts: West Pakistan (present-day Pakistan) and East Pakistan (present-day Bangladesh).

While both, East and West Pakistan practised Islam, they were traditionally, culturally, socially, and linguistically very different groups of people. The forty-five million people of West Pakistan spoke many languages and dialects such as Punjabi and Urdu, whereas the fifty-five million people of East Pakistan spoke only Bangla. Their education system and literature were purely rooted in Bangla.

When talks of one state language, namely Urdu, started circulating, literary activist and educationist, Mohammad Abul Kashem started preparing for what would eventually become a long-drawn battle to protect their mother tongue.

How could there be only one official state language when there was such a vast difference between the eastern and western regions?

He saw Bangla as a source of strength and connection for them. He roped in his friends, Syed Nazrul Islam and Shamsul Alam, to establish Tamaddun Majlish, an organization that supported the Bangla Language Movement.

Through this organization, Abul Kashem and his friends spread awareness about Bangla, its rich literary background, and how important it was for them to have Bangla as a state language.

But most people dismissed them and their opinions. They thought it was an unrealistic move to have two state languages in one country and were scared to support the proposal. People were just happy to have their own independent Pakistan—most were willing to forgo their mother language too!

But not Kashem and his followers—they believed it was outrageous to even think like that. In November 1947, Fazlur Rehman, the then-education minister of Pakistan made an announcement that Bangla would be dropped from many of the approved subjects. According to the new syllabus, there were nine languages, which included Latin and Sanskrit, but there was no Bangla on the list!

Other discriminatory moves against Bangla were printing currency, money orders, railway tickets, etc. only in English and Urdu. These new developments only added fuel to the fire.

The members of Tamaddun Majlish moved from strength to strength to garner support for the language movement.

They held meetings with influential people. They collected thousands of signatures from dignitaries and others and submitted a bill to the government to make Bangla the state language. Students and educationists staged protests at the Dhaka University.

But success seemed distant, until 21 March 1948.

The Dhaka Racecourse was packed to the rafters. Over 5,00,000 women, children, men, and students, young and old, waited with bated breath to see and listen to the Founding Father of Pakistan, Quaid-e-Azam Mohammad Ali Jinnah—their eyes affixed on the eighteen-feet-high rostrum before them. The ground erupted into a cheer for the governor general and the East Pakistan government welcomed him with a scented and colourful shower of rose petals as he walked up towards the rostrum dressed in his karakul cap and a crisp white sherwani in all aplomb, military protection in tow.

He spoke to the crowd about many things—the Partition, the plight of the people of the Punjab and Bengal, the mass exodus of minority Hindus from Pakistan and then, the giant looming subject of the state language arose.

Jinnah's speech stunned the half million people watching him. All doubts were laid to rest when the ground echoed with Jinnah's piercing words, 'But let me make it clear to you that the state language of Pakistan is going to be Urdu and no other language. Anyone who tries to mislead you is merely the enemy of Pakistan. Without one state language, no nation can remain tied up solidly together and function. Look at the history of other countries. Therefore, so far as the state language is concerned, Pakistan's language should be Urdu.'

Jinnah's insensitive speech and complete disregard for the Bangla language, culture, and heritage left the students of East Pakistan enraged. Their resolve to make Bangla the state language only became stronger. The movement gained momentum over the next few years and there were protests all over the eastern province of Pakistan to preserve Bangla.

Khwaja Nazimuddin, Jinnah's successor as governor general, also maintained that Urdu would be the state language at an address in Dhaka on 27 Jan 1952.

When Abul Kashem and his supporters realized that nothing was helping, on 21 February 1952, they decided to hold peaceful student protests across the state. But the government cited Section 144, which prohibited public gatherings of more than three people in one place and tried to squash the protests.

The students were determined. A group of schoolgirls were the first to defy this curb—society stopped girls from participating in such rallies. Alongside the male students, they peacefully marched on to show their love for Bangla. Sadly, the police indiscriminately opened fire at unarmed students as they left the Dhaka University gates onto the streets, killing, injuring, and arresting many of them.

The people of East Pakistan were not going to take this lying down. They were furious and agitated, and they protested the killings of innocent students in the days to follow. A Shaheed Minar, or Martyr's Memorial, was erected at the spot where the students lost their lives to acknowledge their sacrifice for the Bangla language. This small victory had come at a huge price.

The students themselves erected the 10.5 feet high and 6 feet wide Shaheed Minar in a single day after seeking support for raw materials from the local panchayat sardars. They fixed a handwritten placard to the monument saying, 'Shahid Smritistambha'. Abul Kalam Shamsuddin, the editor of the *Daily Azad*, inaugurated the memorial on 26 February 1952. However, the insensitive West Bengal police demolished the memorial three days later.

The police could demolish the memorial but not the memories of the slain martyrs. People across East Pakistan erected similar models of the memorial across the country, especially within educational institutes.

Seeing the ardent fervour of the students and the state-wide outrage, the government finally gave in and announced Bangla as the state language of East Pakistan. Urdu would continue to be the state language of West Pakistan.

Over the years, the Bangla Language Movement grew into a much bigger emotion—an emotion to be free in every way. The freedom to practice their own culture and to be respected. Eventually, after a spate of protests, armed conflicts, and wars (the Bangladesh Liberation War), Bangladesh was born in 1971.

The Bangla Language Movement was not just about a language. It was about one's right to speak in their mother tongue. It was about the identity of more than fifty-five million people who not just spoke and wrote in one language, but even thought and ideated through it. It was the fight to survive discrimination, repression and supremacy based on language and culture.

In 1999, UNESCO acknowledged the sacrifices of the students and citizens of Bangladesh in the Bangla Language Movement and declared Ekushey February or 21 February as World Mother Language Day.

THE BULTOO REVOLUTION

The Story of the Revitalization of a Tribal Language

It had been over five months since the halls of a government school in a remote village in Chhattisgarh wore a haunted look. The chatter and laughter of the kids were conspicuous by its absence. The government-subsidized rice for mid-day meals had not yet reached schools where children from the marginalized poor families in Chhattisgarh's tribal belt studied. They had no clean water to drink, thanks to missing handpumps. But a local man from the area who wanted to report these problems to the authorities, had no way to go about it. He only knew his mother language Gondi and couldn't communicate with officers-in-charge, who mainly spoke in Telugu or Hindi.

'Have you heard of Bultoo Radio of CGNet Swara?' a friend asked him. His friend explained that he just needed to call a toll-free number from his mobile phone and record his story. A reporter or journalist, who knew Gondi, would listen to his story, verify it, and translate it for more people to understand the issue. The man could not believe what he had just heard.

He recorded his story from his phone, not knowing whether anyone would respond to it. Soon, someone from Mumbai heard his message and was so pained by the problem, she did everything in her capacity to ensure that food reached the children and a new handpump was installed near the school. About two weeks later, there was a response to his message on Swara that mid-day meals would finally resume and children would have access to clean drinking water.

All thanks to Bultoo.

The Bultoo Radio service, also known as CGNet Swara or Central Gondwana Network Voice, is a revolutionary radio service for the Gondi tribe. This problem and several other problems that the Adivasis face—unemployment, lack of electricity, financial and land issues, local crimes, human rights, healthcare etc.—would have never been heard if not for CGNet Swara.

CGNet Swara is not just any radio service. It is the voice of the millions of tribes known as Gonds or Koiturs, who live in the dense forest belt of central India, known as Gondwanaland, which comprises of six states: Andhra

Pradesh, Chhattisgarh, Madhya Pradesh, Maharashtra, Odisha, and Telangana. The language they speak is known as Gondi, a language belonging to the Dravidian language family, which is the ancestor of languages such as Tamizh, Telugu, Kannada, and Malayalam.

Swara, started by Shubhranshu Choudhary, an award-winning journalist who has worked extensively with the BBC, has been a blessing for the millions of tribals who live in forest areas and who are completely disconnected with the rest of the world. But why is this?

The answer lies with their language: Gondi.

The 100 million tribals speak languages that the rest of the country do not understand. At about twelve million, the Gond tribe is the largest tribe in our country (13.45–14 per cent), with over three million Gondi speakers.

Post-Independence, when India was divided into states based on linguistic boundaries, the entire Gond tribe was split across multiple states, dividing the tribe by languages. Now one Gondi language was split into six dialects of Gondi. For instance, the Gondis in Maharashtra spoke Marathi-Gondi, those in Andhra spoke Telugu-Gondi, and so on.

Did you know that according to the 2011 census, Hindi has fifty-seven officially recognized varieties, and Hindi is also

one of the varieties? The standard variety of Hindi that everyone speaks, and writes, is known as Khari Boli.

Furthermore, each state had one majority community that spoke a dominant language. This language became the official state language or *rajyabhasha*. The medium of instruction in schools and communication in the government was in the state language. All other languages spoken by the minority communities in that state were conveniently ignored. There was no education in their language, which meant that most of them could not go to school. Even if they had access to a school, they were forced to study in the state language and speak in that language too. As a result, entire generations have nearly forgotten their mother tongue because they have no one to speak with in that language, except with the elderly at home.

Many linguists assert that such an imposition of a language that is not one's own leads to language death and is a crime against humanity.

How could these tribes, not recognized even by the government, solve their problems if they were unable to communicate with anyone? No reporter or journalist could understand their language and, hence, they were unable to share the plight of these poorest of poor tribes in the media—one of the chief reasons why no one knows the true stories of the lives led by millions of Adivasis. The state's denial to allow them easy access to the most basic education and their inability to write in Gondi further aggravated the matter.

Shubhranshu thought, what the pen could not achieve, the voice could. He believed that the strength of the people was in their voices. If they got an opportunity to share their stories on a platform that could be accessible by everyone, and that too in their own languages, they would be able to reach out to anyone to share their grievances, sing songs, narrate folk tales, and do so much more! Also, mobile internet was not only more accessible, but it was also way more affordable than owning a computer or depending on electricity that was far from reliable.

In a nutshell, Shubhranshu had embarked on a journey to democratize journalism where everyone could report their stories with complete freedom, without the fear of being harmed. The portal would eventually become a database of oral communication in the Gondi language.

Armed with a revolutionary idea and engineering support from the team at Microsoft Research, Shubhranshu founded and created the CGNet Swara web portal in 2010. Over time, CGNet Swara became a movement. On an average, the portal receives over 500 calls a day and hundreds of thousands of grievances have been addressed to date. Taking things one step further, the team has even built the first version of a Machine Translation Tool for Gondi, which has demonstrated a 62 per cent accuracy in translation. A Unicode Gondi font that can be used to write from digital devices will also soon be a reality.

The efforts for the revitalization of Gondi didn't just end with the award-winning Bultoo Radio service. Senior Gondi speakers from the six states the tribe is spread across got together under the able leadership of Prof. K.M. Metry to create a Gondi dictionary called *Gondwana Koytoor Gondi Gotti*—a dictionary that would standardize its many dialects. They believe that if Gondi is standardized, chances that the government would make Gondi a part of the Eighth Schedule of our Constitution would be much higher.

Did you know that two Adivasi languages, Bodo (spoken mainly in Assam and Meghalaya), and Santhali (spoken mainly in West Bengal, Jharkhand, and Odisha) were added to the Eighth Schedule in 2004, taking the total number of official languages to twenty-two?

Over four years, they created an exhaustive and comprehensive list of words to create a single standardized variant of Gondi. The team succeeded in building a dictionary with nearly 3500 Gondi words in 2018, overcoming hurdles such as the lack of a proper writing system in Gondi and the absence of any form of Gondi literature. Since 21 July was the first day that they met for their mission to create a Gondi dictionary, 21 July is celebrated as Gondi Language Day every year. Since then, children's books in Gondi and bilingual books in both Gondi and Hindi have been published. In some places, Gondi is also the medium of instruction for primary education.

While Gondi is primarily written in the Devanagari and Telugu scripts, there are two indigenous Gondi scripts — one script was created by Munshi Mangal Singh Masaram in 1918, and the other script is known as the Gunjala script or the Gunjala Gondi Lipi that was discovered in the Adilabad district of Telangana.

For Adivasis, there's always been a tussle between being true to their identity and culture through their language while also learning the dominant language of the state for better job opportunities and a better life.

A volunteer at CGNet Swara said that it was now important for the tribes to know Gondi if they wanted government jobs—an incentive for the tribes to learn their language.

The fight to keep the language alive is real and it hasn't been easy. There are many more resilient and dedicated language warriors like Shubhranshu Chowdhary, such as Acharya Motiravan Kangale, a Gond religious teacher and the founder of 'Akhil Gondwana Gondi Sahitya Parishad' (All-Gondwana Gondi Literary Academy) who has not only captured Gondi cultures and traditions in his books but also written comprehensive Hindi to Gondi and Gondi to Hindi thesaurus among other noted works. Prof. Dr G. Manoja and Prof. V. Krishna from the Palamuru University in Telangana are translating the Gondi manuscripts found in Gunjala script. Veer Keram is a part of the Endangered Language Documentation Project and works to promote the use of Gondi through social media. Sher Singh Achla, aged seventy-five, not only teaches Gondi to school children but tours all of Chhattisgarh to propagate the use of Gondi and the setting up of Gondi libraries. Kamalabai, who is aged ninety-five, has educated and raised three generations of people who can speak in Gondi and understand and write the Gunjala script. These are only a few, among so many others, who are the torchbearers in this long but hopeful struggle of language revival.

THE VOICE OF THE BRAVE

The Story of How Nepali Became India's Official Language

There were celebrations in many parts of Darjeeling, West Bengal, on 20 August. The Gorkha Ranga Mancha and the Town Hall were lit up with lamps and diyas. Women in sarees and kurtas and men in daura-suruwal suits rallied till the Ranga Mancha. The Town Hall was redolent with the aroma of authentic Nepali dishes. A dais was set up to felicitate musicians, writers, and prominent figures who had made significant contributions to Nepali culture, literature, and the Nepali language movement or Nepali Bhasa Andolan.

20 August 1992 was an important day for the Nepali speakers of India. Finally, after thirty-six years of fighting for their rights, Nepali was recognized as an official language in our Constitution. This day is observed every

year as the Nepali Language Recognition Day or Nepali Bhasa Manyata Divas.

It all started when the British East India Company established Darjeeling during their colonial rule in India as a part of Sikkim.

The beautiful state of Sikkim was surrounded by Nepal in the west, Bhutan in the east, India in the south, and China in the north. Nepal always wanted Sikkim to be a part of its provinces. This strategically located state was sought after by both, the British and Nepal, and they both battled hard to make it their own.

For the British, controlling Sikkim not only meant an easy and commanding entrance into Nepal and Bhutan—a strong defence post in the Himalayas—but also an enchanting summer resort for the Britishers who wanted to escape the heat of India.

The Gorkha Kingdom of Nepal also had its eyes on Sikkim for its strategic location. They attacked Sikkim for many years and finally, in 1780, they managed to seize it from under the British rule. With British Sikkim, the Nepali Gorkhas also got Darjeeling. Sikkim was under the Nepalese rule for almost forty years.

The Gorkhas did not stop at that. They kept attacking the northern frontier to capture more territories, but the British were never going to give up on these enchanting

Himalayan territories, which also served as a trade route and gateway to Tibet and China.

The tug of war for Sikkim between the British and the Gorkhas continued. The British captured Sikkim back from Nepal in the Anglo-Nepal war that broke out in 1814. As a part of the victory, the British signed a treaty with the Gorkhas (Treaty of Sugauli, 1815), whereby Nepal had to give back all the territories they had captured from the Raja of Sikkim to the East India Company.

A couple of years later, in 1817, in another treaty (Treaty of Titalia), the British reinstated the Raja of Sikkim who ruled Sikkim before these wars had broken out. Sikkim was now a buffer state between Nepal, Tibet, and Bhutan, which is like a small independent country situated between more powerful countries.

However, ten years on, a battle between Sikkim and the Gorkhas erupted again. The British did not want to let go of Darjeeling. The British officer, General Lloyd, managed to convince the Raja of Sikkim to give them Darjeeling. The Raja could not afford to be enemies with the British and, in 1835, Darjeeling was granted to the British East India Company.

The British developed the Darjeeling region. Infrastructure such as roads, railway, homes, hotels, schools, and hospitals were built. Tea estates burgeoned.

Soon, Darjeeling became a tourist attraction and was known as the 'Queen of Hills'. Post-Independence, Darjeeling became a part of West Bengal.

In the battles that raged between the British and Nepal, it was the Gorkhas who were caught in the crossfire. The Gorkhas were always second to none—the stories of their bravery are sung even today. Despite the many battles, the British always admired the Gorkhas for their bravery and spirit to fight and recruited them in their army. It is said that over 100,000 Gorkhas fought in World War I!

Many recruited Gorkhas eventually settled in Assam, Darjeeling, Kalimpong, and Kurseong regions of northern West Bengal, giving rise to newer generations of Indian Gorkhas. These Nepali-speaking Gorkhas of Indian origin are referred to as Gorkhalis—Gorkhas who are proud of their Nepali heritage, yet Indian in every way. However, they found themselves amid the huge Bengali-speaking population of West Bengal.

The Gorkhalis have clearly been victims of an identity crisis for a very long time. Unlike the eight million Nepali citizens living in India at present, they were actually Indian. But since nationals from both countries are free to migrate between the borders and settle in either country, they're often confused for being migrant Nepalis and the local population sees them as outsiders—those that don't belong to India.

Every attempt has been made to suppress the Gorkhalis and one of the best ways to target any culture is to attack the use of its language. According to the 2011 census, there are more than three million Nepali-speaking people in India. In a bid to avoid making Nepali a medium of instruction in Gorkhali-dominant regions such as Darjeeling, the West Bengal government made sincere efforts to show that the Nepali-speaking Gorkhalis in Darjeeling were a minority in the region. This was done to make Bengali the compulsory medium of instruction in schools.

The West Bengal government also tried to impose the use of Bengali in public spaces. In Darjeeling, one could see instructions and advertisements on hoardings in Bengali and English. Government forms and any other application forms were also issued only in Bengali and English but not in Nepali or even Hindi. In the wake of all this injustice, a language movement to honour the Nepali language was imminent.

The Indian Gorkhas living in all parts of the country began demanding that Nepali be made an official language of India. In 1956, Anand Singh Thapa, the editor of a Nepali daily, *Jagrat Gorkha*, led this movement. He urged Dr Rajendra Prasad, independent India's president to take cognizance of the grave injustice meted out to Gorkhalis and give the Nepali language the respect it deserved by adding it to the Indian Constitution. The erasure of their language by the takeover of Bengali had to be addressed.

Some headway was made in 1961, when Nepali was recognized as the sixth official language of West Bengal. But this was not what the Gorkhalis fought for. They wanted Nepali to be made an official language of India because Nepali speakers were scattered across many states, not just West Bengal. Many organizations were formed to support the movement and the peaceful Nepali Bhasa Andolan gained momentum. Committees were formed, meetings were held, articles and Nepali literature were published

Finally, on 20 August 1992, a bill was passed in the Parliament, and Nepali was declared as an official language of India. Now, any Indian citizen could use Nepali as their mother tongue, use it for trade and business, and the Indian Government would also take measures to preserve and protect the Nepali language. Konkani and Meitei (Manipuri) were also included in the Eighth Schedule in 1992.

While this was a milestone victory for the Gorkhalis and the entire Nepali-speaking population of India, situation at the ground level did not see much change. Bengali continued to be imposed. Education was chiefly in English and Bengali, and the Gorkhalis were still treated as immigrants.

The only way to end this was by having a separate state: Gorkhaland. While the Gorkhalis have been asking for separate statehood since the early 1900s, the demand for it has intensified over the years. The Gorkhaland Territorial Administration (GTA), a semi-autonomous body that gives the Gorkhalis some rights to govern Darjeeling and other hilly areas of West Bengal was established in 2012. This gives them an opportunity to establish the true identity of Gorkhas through socio-economic growth, infrastructure, education, culture and language development.

As with every other language, the inevitable continues to happen with Nepali as well—more and more speakers are steering themselves towards learning dominant languages such as Hindi and English for better job opportunities. The world is going digital and digital interfaces and applications are mainly in English. And this language shift will continue to happen till there are jobs demanding the knowledge of Nepali. But the sliver of hope lies with the Nepali language and literature enthusiasts, and the Gorkhalis who celebrate the Nepali Bhasa Manyata Divas with pomp, ensuring that the love and loyalty towards their language thrives.

Many other language movements like the Nepali Bhasa Andolan have taken place across the world—be it the First Afrikaans Language movement in the Republic of South Africa, the Gaelic Revival Movement in Ireland, the Meitei Language Movement for recognition of the Manipuri language, Meitei, or the Bangla Language Movement in East Pakistan (now Bangladesh). These movements will continue to happen because within any language lies the cultural wisdom and true identity of its speakers. While it's not certain if India will create one more state of Gorkhaland, movements such as these protect and preserve languages and cultures from a certain death.

THREE MEN ON A RAFT

The Story of India's Hidden Indigenous Language

In early 2008, three men boarded a raft to cross a small but gushing mountain river, which would take them to a remote village known as Kichang in the one Indian state where even Indians need a permit to visit—Arunachal Pradesh. This village is home to the indigenous Aka tribes. They were there to study and record the lesser-known languages, Aka and Miji.

Kichang was barcly a village then, with just four bamboo houses on stilts. They entered a house where two women sat in a veranda. One of the women, Kachim, began to speak as their camera rolled. Kachim narrated her life's story to them.

But it was not what they expected. The language was different. It wasn't Aka or Miji. It was different compared to either of them. The nouns, the verbs, the meanings, all different. They looked at each other, absolutely bewildered at what they had found.

It was Koro, a language no one ever knew existed. And the videotape in their possession was the first ever recording of that hidden language.

According to Dr David Harrison, one of the three people on this expedition alongside Gregory Anderson and Ganesh Murmu, no one knows exactly how many languages are spoken in Arunachal Pradesh. Especially because India does not officially recognize any language that has less than 10,000 speakers. These languages are either merged with other major language groups or groups that are little over 10,000 but are culturally similar, completely ignoring the fact that their languages are distinctively different. Koro was one of them.

It is believed that Koro is a Tibeto-Burman language that belongs to the Sino-Tibetan language family (which has about 400 languages). Koro is spoken by the Aka tribe, which has two main sub-tribes—Hruso and Koro.

As of 2022, there are 1500 to 2000 Koro speakers in India.

The speakers of Koro have a unique way of living, celebrating festivals, recording births and deaths, cooking food, growing vegetables and so on. The language contains the wisdom of the local environment in its unique vocabulary. This includes names of the animals, birds, insects, plants, trees that are endemic to that region. If Koro goes extinct, the knowledge of all these things and more would become extinct with it too.

But why was Koro hidden from the world all these years? The reasons why indigenous languages remain hidden from the world are manifold—they are unrecorded, undocumented, and have been non-existent because people choose to hide them! Just like the language Toto spoken by a little over 1600 people living in the district of Jalpaiguri in northern West Bengal, very close to the India-Bhutan border. The people speak Toto only at home; while outside, they speak in Nepali and they write in Bengali, which is the medium of instruction in their schools.

According to linguists and researchers who have devoted their lives to studying human geography, their lives, their tongues, it is quite possible that these indigenous tribes *choose* to remain hidden from the world, from the fear of being ostracized by society for not choosing a mainstream language they cannot identify with.

Instead, like Hijra Farsi and other languages we've read about in this book, they only speak in this hidden language with their fellow speakers who share their tongue and in private. They see themselves as custodians of their culture and want to protect it.

It's also likely that Koro was ignored by local authorities and governing bodies who promised to support the tribe and preserve their language but shied away only to show their support for mainstream tribes. The 1500-odd Koro-speaking Aka tribespeople were absorbed into the society of the larger Aka tribe that spoke Hruso.

The government does not recognize the Koro-speaking population as a different and distinct ethnic tribe. They are not part of the Indian census nor are they registered as a proper tribe in the official report of the *Linguistic Survey of India*. It means that there will be no books written in Koro, no education in Koro, no official documents in Koro, no true recognition of their rich past, no acknowledgement of their very existence.

In February 2020, the United Nations (UN) declared the decade 2022–2032 as the International Decade of Indigenous Languages, to focus on the indigenous language users' rights and work on the empowerment of these tribes. This is known as the Los Pinos Declaration and it emphasizes indigenous peoples' rights to freedom of expression, to an education in their mother tongue, and to participation in public life using their languages as prerequisites for the survival of indigenous languages, many of which are currently on the verge of extinction.

At least one language of the 7000+ languages documented in the world goes extinct every two weeks, and close to half of these 7000+ languages are endangered or on the brink of extinction. Koro is one of the lucky languages that has been recorded and documented, thanks to the three men on the raft. More work is being done to fully comprehend the mystery surrounding Koro and keep it from becoming extinct, as has happened with many other indigenous languages that have vanished from the face of the earth without ever being recorded.

The local ministers are trying to convince the government to acknowledge and support the use of Koro for the Aka tribe, but little is being done. There are dedicated individuals such as Khandu Degio, Bachi Degio, Babung Chijang, and Dorjee Degio, among others, who are working to conserve the language through the creation of pictorial and verbal dictionaries. Children and newborns are introduced to Koro right away. While Koro does not have any script, they have borrowed the Hruso script and are working towards adapting it for Koro. This is because of the phonetic similarities between the two languages, Hruso and Koro. Khandu, whose mother speaks Hruso-Aka and father, Koro-Aka, suggests that most Koro-Aka speakers are multilingual, knowing how to speak Koro, Hruso, and even Hindi and English.

And what better way to keep a language alive than through folktales and songs? The Koro-Aka tribe has unique cultures, traditions, and rituals they follow, and they have unique songs that are sung for each of their ceremonies. They hope that these songs will be sung by their generation and dream that their stories will be retold across generations to help keep the language alive.

Three men on a raft accidentally discovered Koro. There could be many such hidden languages still being whispered within the four walls of a home, still lived on the many indigenous tongues of our country, until someone comes along and accidentally discovers them.

LANGUAGES MUST SURVIVE

Every language has a story, and every story has a language. The stories in this book tell us that languages are living entities. They are born, they grow, they change, and many of them perish over time. But many of them survive too, thanks to the selfless and persevering efforts of hundreds of language activists, conservationists, and reformists who have dedicated their lives to the preservation and revitalization of vulnerable, endangered, and even extinct languages.

We need languages and the languages need us. The sign language is one such language. According to the WHO (World Health Organization), over sixty-three million Indians suffer from hearing and speech impairments and of these, over fifty lakh are children alone. The sign language is central to their survival in a world that's communicating at micro levels. An appeal has been made to the central government to add the Indian Sign Language (ISL) to the existing twenty-two official languages in the Eighth Schedule of our Constitution. This will aid the establishment of more schools for the deaf and mute, assuring them better jobs and a good quality of life. However, this is taking time because we are a very diverse country and every culture has their unique signs and gestures. The government is working towards standardizing it before making it official.

ISLRTC (Indian Sign Language Research and Training Centre) released the first digital Indian Sign Language Dictionary on 23 March 2018 at India International Centre, New Delhi. Consisting of 3000 terms, it contains signs for everyday use and displays their corresponding meanings in English and Hindi. The dictionary is now in its third edition with 10,000 terms (launched in 2021) and is a blessing for interpreters, parents, teachers, and children.

Movements, organizations, stories like these are important because they give people hope. No matter how many language shifts happen in our society, for all the reasons we've read about in the book, it is up to us to not allow our mother languages to weather and erode and replace all our indigenous knowledge with global languages.

There's much at stake. The only way they can survive is if we continue to have conversations, share stories, and sing songs in tongues that are our own.

AUTHOR'S NOTE

'*Kem chho*, Vaishali *ben*?'

I was startled to read this message on my phone. That too, someone saying, 'How are you, Vaishali?' in my mother tongue, Gujarati, in the wee hours of my frantic Mumbai morning.

No, it wasn't anyone among my family or friends. No, it wasn't anyone who was a Gujarati by miles! He was a Russian scholar who had dedicated three years of his life to understanding and learning Parsi Gujarati! After speaking to many Parsi and Irani friends in Mumbai when working on this book, I found the answers I was looking for with a Russian scholar who shared his research resources with a complete stranger—me—without any questions asked. It was enough for him to know that I wanted to share the true story behind the Parsi language with children and adults alike.

And this is just one of the behind-the-scenes encounters I had while researching for this book.

The making of *Taatung Tatung and Other Amazing Stories of India's Diverse Languages* has been nothing short of remarkable. Just like its stories. While the book speaks to everyone in many tongues, it says only one thing—let the languages live. These stories cover languages that are being spoken or were once spoken across the length and breadth of our country.

And I live in Mumbai. How could I write about languages spoken in the north-eastern tip of India and those that are being spoken in the deepest forests in central India while sitting at my cluttered desk in a Mumbai home? How could I be certain that everything I wrote was not only accurate but also as relevant and as current as possible?

Of course, I had the internet at my fingertips. I could type whatever questions I had about any language and the internet threw back some really interesting pieces of information and trivia, which helped me a great deal in writing many of the stories. Not only that, as I dug deeper into that rabbit hole, I even discovered stories about languages I never knew existed. Like Koro, Hijra Farsi, Toto, and Brahui, among so many others.

But how authentic were these resources? What if that information was true but dated? I had to be absolutely sure and careful about every word I was adding to the book.

From experience, I know that some of the most fascinating bits of information and some of the coolest anecdotes that are not published anywhere lie only with subject matter experts. In my case, these subject matter experts were diverse, just like our languages—from linguists, to archaeologists, to historians, to language warriors, activists, educators, and even our own tribespeople. The stories in this book echo the lives of our countryfolk.

I was fortunate to meet some amazing people on my journey who shared valuable information about their languages with me. I had some of the most bizarre experiences and I made some truly special friends along the way, but above all, with every new person I spoke to, my respect for our cultural and linguistic diversity grew in leaps and bounds.

While a Russian expert told me more about Parsi, a speaker and language activist shared some of the most beautiful stories about Koro, a language spoken by only about 1500 people on this planet. While I spoke to an award-winning journalist and local tribes from Chhattisgarh to learn more about Gondi, it was an archaeologist who told me more about the Brahmi script.

After reading many books on our linguistic diversity and doing a course on the History of Indian Languages and

Scripts, I was almost scared of writing this book because there were some mighty shoes to fill. I had to do the languages, their speakers, and their protectors justice.

And I hope I have achieved that with every story.

Thank you.

BIBLIOGRAPHY

1. Books and Journal Articles

Abbi, Anvita. *Voices from the Lost Horizon: Stories and Songs of the Great Andamanese*. New Delhi: Niyogi Books, 2021.

Abbi, Anvita, et. al. 'Where Have All the Speakers Gone? A Sociolinguistic Study of the Great Andamanese.' *Indian Linguistics* 68.3-4 (2007): 325–343, accessed 8 December 2022, http://www.andamanese.net/paper_Indian%20Linguistics_2007.pdf.

Ahmad, Waheed, ed. 'Address by Muhammad Ali Jinnah, Governor General of Pakistan, in Dacca, East Pakistan: 21 March 1948.' *The Nation's Voice, Vol. VII: Launching the State and the End of the Journey (Aug. 1947–Sept. 1948)*. Karachi: Quaid-i-Azam Academy, 2003, pp. 243–258, accessed 8 December 2022, http://www.columbia.edu/itc/mealac/pritchett/00islamlinks/txt_jinnah_dacca_1948.html.

Awan, Muhammad Safeer, and Muhammad Sheeraz. 'Queer but Language: A Sociolinguistic Study of Farsi.' *International Journal of Humanities and Social Science* 1.10 (2011): 127–135, accessed 8 December 2022, https://www.ijhssnet.com/journals/Vol_1_No_10_August_2011/17.pdf.

Degawan, Minnie. 'Indigenous Languages: Knowledge and Hope.' *The UNESCO Courier* 1 (2019): 7, accessed 9 December 2022, https://en.unesco.org/sites/default/files/cou_1_19_en.pdf.

Devy, G.N., and Abhay Flavian Xaxa, ed. *Being Adivasi: Existence, Entitlements, Exclusion.* Rethinking India series. New Delhi: Vintage, 2021.

Faruqi, Shamsur Rahman. *Early Urdu Literary Culture.* New Delhi: Oxford University Press, 2001, accessed 5 December 2022, http://www.columbia.edu/itc/mealac/pritchett/00fwp/srf/earlyurdu/01chap01.pdf.

Harrison, K. David. *The Last Speakers: The Quest to Save the World's Most Endangered Languages.* Washington, D.C.: National Geographic, 2010.

Joshi, Jagat Pati, and Asko Parpola, ed. *Corpus of Indus Seals and Inscriptions.* Helsinki: Suomalainen Tiedeakatemia, 1987, accessed 8 December 2022, https://ignca.gov.in/Asi_data/76884.pdf.

Lorea, Carola Erika. 'Bengali Settlers in the Andaman Islands: The Performance of Homeland.' *The Newsletter* 77 Summer (2017): 4–5, https://www.iias.asia/sites/iias/files/theNewsletter/2019-06/IIAS_NL77_FULL.pdf.

Mohan, Peggy Ramesar. *Wanderers, Kings, Merchants: The Story of India through Its Languages*. New Delhi: Penguin Random House India, 2021.

Murthy, N.S.R. 'The History of English Education in India: A Brief Study.' *Journal for Research Scholars and Professionals of English Language Teaching* 2.10 (2018): 1–7, accessed 9 December 2022, https://www.jrspelt.com/wp-content/uploads/2018/11/Murthy-Education-in-India.pdf.

Ravishankar, T.S. 'Six Decades of Indian Epigraphy (1950–2010): Sanskrit and Dravidian Inscriptions.' *Ancient India, New Series* 1 (2011): 261–292, accessed 8 December 2022, https://asi.nic.in/Ancient_India/recent_issues/new_series_1/article_10.pdf.

2. Newspaper and Magazine Articles

Banerji, Annie. 'Indian State Bans Unnecessary Surgery on Intersex Babies.' *Reuters*. 28 August 2019, https://www.reuters.com/article/india-lgbt-intersex-idUSL5N25O22X.

Barbora, Madhumita. 'The Language of the Seven Sisters.' *The ACU Review*. 6 December 2019, https://www.acu.ac.uk/the-acu-review/the-languages-of-the-seven-sisters/#:~:text=In%20the%20state%20of%20Assam,it%20is%20Mizo%20and%20English.

Bhambhri, C.P. 'Withering of Language-based States.' *The Economic Times*. 16 January 2010, https://economictimes.indiatimes.com/opinion/et-

commentary/withering-of-language-based-states/
articleshow/5450588.cms.

Bhutia, Sherab Palden. 'Constitutional Recognition of Nepali Language in India: A Brief Outline.' *Sikkim Chronicle*. 20 August 2021, https://www. thesikkimchronicle.com/constitutional-recognition-of-nepali-language-in-india-a-brief-outline.

Chakrabarti, Angana. 'Ekushe February: When East Pakistan Fought and Died for Victory of Mother Language Bangla.' *The Print*. 21 February 2020, https://theprint.in/world/ekushe-february-when-east-pakistan-fought-died-for-victory-of-mother-language-bangla/368767.

Chari, Mridula. 'How the Map of India Was Redrawn on the Lines of Language.' *Scroll*. 1 November 2016, https://scroll.in/article/820359/how-the-map-india-was-redrawn-on-the-lines-of-language.

Choudhary, Shubhranshu. 'The Miracle of Radio: Bultoo.' *The Wire*. 15 January 2016, https://thewire. in/media/the-miracle-of-radio-bultoo.

Dizikes, Peter. 'The Writing on the Wall.' *MIT News*. 21 February 2018, https://news.mit.edu/2018/humans-speak-through-cave-art-0221.

Gahlot, Mandakini. 'Pondicherry, the French Outpost in India.' *France24*. 18 March 2013, https://www. france24.com/en/20130318-pondicherry-the-French-outpost-in-India.

Gibbens, Sarah. 'Ancient Cave Drawings and Early Human Language Linked in New Study.' *National Geographic*. 22 February 2018, https://www.nationalgeographic.

com/history/article/acoustic-caves-rock-art-language-origin-spd?loggedin=true&rnd=1668055867533.

Goel, Ina. 'India's Third Gender Rises Again.' *Sapiens*. 26 September 2019, https://www.sapiens.org/biology/hijra-india-third-gender.

Gupta, Surbhi. '80 People from Six States Gather with One Aim: A Gondi Dictionary.' *Indian Express*. 25 March 2018, https://indianexpress.com/article/cities/delhi/80-people-from-six-states-gather-with-one-aim-a-gondi-dictionary-5110349.

Jones, Mark. 'Pondicherry: A Corner of India That Is Forever France.' *Independent*. 13 January 2013, https://www.independent.co.uk/travel/asia/pondicherry-a-corner-of-india-that-is-forever-france-8449052.html.

Krishnamachari, Suganthy. 'Decoding the Indus Script.' *The Hindu*. 13 August 2015, https://www.thehindu.com/features/friday-review/history-and-culture/dravidian-proof-of-the-indus-script/article10310982.ece.

Kumar, Anu. 'Thomas Macaulay Won the Debate on How to Shape Indian Education. So Who Were the Losers?' *Scroll*. 4 February 2017, https://scroll.in/magazine/821605/thomas-macaulay-and-the-debate-over-english-education-in-india.

Kumar, Kuldeep. 'Politics of Language in UP Reflects India's History of Favouring Sanskrit over Urdu.' *The Wire*. 3 April 2017, https://thewire.in/politics/the-politics-of-language-in-up-reflects-the-nations-history-of-favouring-sanskrit-over-urdu.

Kundalia, Nidhi Dugar. 'Queer Language.' *The Hindu*. 30 November 2013, https://www.thehindu.com/features/magazine/queer-language/article5407840.ece.

Lasania, Yunus Y. 'Not "Urdu", Not "Hyderabadi Hindi", It's Dakhni: Understanding Our Spoken Language.' *Medium*. 13 June 2020, https://medium.com/@hyderabadhistoryproject/not-urdu-not-hyderabadi-hindi-it-s-dakhni-understanding-our-spoken-language-7520ff4ced06.

Mahadevan, Iravatham. 'An Epigraphic Perspective on the Antiquity of Tamil.' *The Hindu*. 24 June 2010, https://www.thehindu.com/opinion/op-ed/An-epigraphic-perspective-on-the-antiquity-of-Tamil/article16265606.ece.

Mehta, Nitin. 'A Nation Born out of Sanskrit, and Still in Love with It.' *The Daily Guardian*. 17 October 2020, https://thedailyguardian.com/a-nation-born-out-of-sanskrit-and-still-in-love-with-it.

Morrison, Dan. '"Hidden" Language Found in Remote Indian Tribe: Koro Tongue Documented in a Linguistic "black hole".' *National Geographic*. 6 October 2010, https://www.nationalgeographic.com/science/article/101005-lost-language-india-science.

Mukherji, Anahita. 'Hijra Farsi: Secret Language Knits Community.' *The Times of India*. 7 October 2013, https://timesofindia.indiatimes.com/india/hijra-farsi-secret-language-knits-community/articleshow/23618092.cms.

Mukhopadhyay, Nilanjan. 'Past Continuous: How British Imperialism Influenced the Creation of

Linguistic States.' *The Wire*. 10 July 2018, https://
thewire.in/history/states-linguistic-british-
imperialism-india-independence.

Nair, Nandini. 'G.N. Devy: A Portrait of the Linguist
as a Humanist.' *Open*. 17 August 2016, https://
openthemagazine.com/profile-2/gn-devy-a-
portrait-of-the-linguist-as-a-humanist/?fbclid=I
wAR0D42HDDsv1bb_Fh-3PhJlXjgFpmkfbKiE-
h5QTTvW2h3pPnYCxHSzFlTI.

Nathan, Chenthil. 'The History of Anti-Hindi
Imposition Movements in Tamil Nadu.' *The News
Minute*. 4 June 2019, https://www.thenewsminute.
com/article/history-anti-hindi-imposition-
movements-tamil-nadu-102983.

Pillalamarri, Akhilesh. 'The Story of India's Many Scripts.'
The Diplomat. 1 July 2019, https://thediplomat.
com/2019/07/the-story-of-indias-many-scripts.

Phua, Amy. 'How the Dakhni Language Defines Cultural
Intimacy and Regional Belonging.' *The News Minute*.
2 October 2021, https://www.thenewsminute.
com/article/how-dakhni-language-defines-cultural-
intimacy-and-regional-belonging-156006.

Saha, Abhishek. 'The Legacy of Sukapha, Founder of Ahom
Kingdom.' *The Indian Express*. 23 June 2020, https://
indianexpress.com/article/explained/the-legacy-of-
sukapha-founder-of-ahom-kingdom-6468320.

'Full text: This Is What Nathuram Godse Said in His
Defence of Mahatma Gandhi's Assassination.' *India
TV*. 30 January 2016, https://www.indiatvnews.com/

news/india/nathuram-godse-defence-mahatma-gandhi-assassination-57320.html.

'They Helped Build Modern India but Are Shrinking as a People.' *The New York Times*. 3 October 2021, https://www.nytimes.com/2021/10/03/world/asia/india-parsi.html.

'This village in Karnataka speaks only in Sanskrit.' *Conde Nast Traveller*. 25 January 2021, https://www.cntraveller.in/story/mattur-village-karnataka-speaks-sanskrit.

'We Are Walking on a Graveyard of Languages: G.N. Devy.' *Arunachal Times*. 27 March 2018, https://arunachaltimes.in/index.php/2018/03/27/we-are-walking-on-a-graveyard-of-languages-gn-devy.

3. Websites and Other Sources

Chavan, Akshay. 'James Prinsep: Decoding Ancient India.' Live History India. 20 August 2019, https://www.livehistoryindia.com/story/people/james-princep-decoding-ancient-india.

Eduljee, K.E. 'Early Parsi History.' Heritage Institute, accessed 6 December 2022, http://www.heritage institute.com/zoroastrianism/history/qissa2.htm.

Jain, Anshika. 'Shravanabelagola and Its Mauryan Connection.' Live History India. 3 July 2019, https://www.livehistoryindia.com/story/monuments/shravanabelagola-its-mauryan-connection.

Joshi, Nikul. 'Sanskrit.' *WorldHistory.org*. 22 August 2016, https://www.worldhistory.org/Sanskrit.

Macaulay, T.B. 'Minute.' 2 February 1835, http://www.columbia.edu/itc/mealac/pritchett/00generallinks/macaulay/txt_minute_education_1835.html.

Mark, Joshua J. 'Indus Valley Civilization: Definition.' *WorldHistory.org*. 7 October 2020, https://www.worldhistory.org/Indus_Valley_Civilization.

Mukherjee, Sibasis. 'Sindhi Language and Its History.' Researchgate. May 2020, https://www.researchgate.net/publication/341767214_Sindhi_language_and_its_history.

Rahnamoon, Fariborz. 'History of Persian or Parsi Language.' Iran Chamber. 30 November 2022, https://www.iranchamber.com/literature/articles/persian_parsi_language_history.php.

Zykov, Anton. 'Videography-based documentation of the language of Parsis in Gujarat and Maharashtra.' Endangered Languages Archive, accessed 12 December 2022, https://www.elararchive.org/dk0518/

'A Historical Perspective of Urdu.' National Council for Promotion of Urdu Language, Ministry of Education, Govt. of India, accessed 5 December 2022, https://www.urducouncil.nic.in/council/historical-perspective-urdu.

'Discovering the Rock Art of Dr V.S. Wakankar.' Bradshaw Foundation, accessed 8 December 2022, https://www.bradshawfoundation.com/india/dr_vs_wakankar/index.php.

'Historical Background of Andaman.' South Andaman District, accessed 6 December 2022, https://southandaman.nic.in/history.

'Koro Aka Language Documentation Project.' Living Tongues, accessed 8 December 2022, https://livingtongues.org/koro-aka.

'Languages Included in the Eighth Schedule of the Indian Constitution.' Department of Official Language, Govt. of India, accessed 5 December 2022, https://rajbhasha.gov.in/en/languages-included-eighth-schedule-indian-constitution.

'Languages in Andaman and Nicobar Islands.' Maps of India, accessed 6 December 2022, https://www.mapsofindia.com/andaman-nicobar-islands/languages.html.

'Languages in Pondicherry.' Maps of India, accessed 6 December 2022, https://www.mapsofindia.com/pondicherry/languages.html.

'Lisan al-Dawat: The Dawoodi Bohra Language.' The Dawoodi Bohras. 10 December 2021, https://www.thedawoodibohras.com/2021/12/10/lisan-al-dawat-the-language-of-the-dawoodi-bohras.

'Report of the States Reorganization Commission.' 1955, accessed 5 December 2022, https://www.mha.gov.in/sites/default/files/State%20Reorganisation%20Commisison%20Report%20of%201955_270614.pdf.

'The Knowledge of Language.' *Mkgandhi.org*, accessed 5 December 2022, https://www.mkgandhi.org/gandhiji/26language.htm.

'The Official Languages Act, 1963.' Department of Official Language, Govt. of India, accessed 5 December 2022, https://rajbhasha.gov.in/en/official-languages-act-1963.

'Upcoming Decade of Indigenous Languages (2022 – 2032) to Focus on Indigenous Language Users' Human Rights.' UNESCO. 28 February 2020, https://www.unesco.org/en/articles/upcoming-decade-indigenous-languages-2022-2032-focus-indigenous-language-users-human-rights.

4. Additional Websites

https://bharatavani.in/bharatavani
https://www.bhasharesearch.org/introduction.html
http://www.cgnetswara.org/
https://www.ciil.org
https://www.ethnologue.com
https://gndevy.in/index.html
https://livingtongues.org

*Several other sources, along with original research, have been used while writing this book.

ACKNOWLEDGEMENTS

The seeds for this book were sown on a trip to the Bhimbetka Rock Shelters in 2019. The magnificent cave art communicated with me in no particular language. This led me to think about communication and languages in a very different light. That same year, I also travelled to the Indus Valley Civilization site, Dholavira, in Gujarat. The signboard discovered there lay undeciphered. The universe was giving me too many signs to work on books about mysterious languages. Thus began my journey with *Taatung Tatung*.

Through the title of this book, *Taatung Tatung*, I wish to pay tribute to Late Elder Boa Sr, the last speaker of the Great Andamanese language, who sang this song for Prof. Anvita Abbi's path-breaking documentation project to protect and preserve marginalized voices— Voices of the Great Andamanese or VOGA. It is a mark of respect for our extinct languages and the last speakers of all the languages we have lost.

The workshop on Indian languages, conducted by noted linguist and polyglot, Raamesh Gowri Raghavan, for INSTUCEN (Indian Study Centre) in Mumbai, helped me tremendously to understand many aspects of known and unknown languages. I'd like to extend my deepest gratitude to Raamesh sir for his time and knowledge that he shared so generously with me.

Thank you, Shubhranshu Choudhary, for being such an inspiration with your remarkable efforts for the revitalization of Gondi and for helping me to write the all-important story about the preservation of tribal languages.

Khandu Degio, without your support, I would not have been able to write the story of Koro-Aka. Thank you for the continued work that you do for Living Tongues Institute of Endangered Languages and for sharing your priceless research and resources with me.

Never did I imagine that a Russian would help me with information on Parsi Gujarati. Ever so grateful to you, Anton Zykov, for sharing your brilliant research on Parsi Gujarati with me, that you accomplished with the support of ELDP (Endangered Language Documentation Programme). *Mara khoob khoob aabhaar.*

Ganesh N. Devy, immensely grateful to you, sir, for your insightful research papers, articles, and talks, which have been a source of inspiration throughout my journey. Thank you for taking the time to read my manuscript and looking at it with a critical lens, while encouraging me to not give up in my pursuit to educate young readers about the significance of our indigenous languages.

My deepest gratitude for the very respected linguist and scholar of minority languages, Padma Shri Prof. Anvita Abbi, whose work has been nothing short of awe-inspiring for me. Thank you, Ms Abbi, for reading my manuscript, suggesting some critical updates, and for letting me know that this book matters if we want our languages, cultures, and the collective wisdom they bring, to survive.

Grateful to you, Peggy Mohan, for your precious time, for looking at my manuscript critically, and for sharing your wisdom and knowledge with me on the history of our languages, especially Sanskrit.

Thank you, Kalika Bali, for not only taking the time to read my manuscript at such a short notice on a personal vacation, but also responding to it with a beautiful and encouraging email that made every word in this book count.

Much gratitude to Nagmani for telling me more about the life of Gonds, and to Nethi Sai Kiran, a Wikimedian working on Gondi and Kolami languages, for sharing the Gondi script with me and reading the chapter on Gondi for accuracy.

Shashi Tharoor, special thanks to you, sir, for giving my manuscript your valuable time, for reading it, and for sharing words of encouragement and hope for this book. Indeed, I'm truly humbled and honoured by your kind support.

This book would not have been possible without my talented editor, Smit Zaveri, who worked hard with me to ensure that the narratives and stories are powerful. Thank you, Smit, for your constructive and objective criticism on every aspect of the book, for the systematic edits, and for helping me realize my vision.

My publisher, Sohini Mitra, has been with me every step of the way. My heartfelt gratitude to you, Sohini, and to Penguin, for giving me the opportunity to create this book and for extending your kind support to me throughout my journey.

Sushmita Chatterjee, thank you for being with me throughout the critical last mile of the journey, for helping me polish my manuscript for correctness and accuracy, and for giving me the much-needed confidence that we're working on something very exciting indeed!

A big thank you, Adrija Ghosh, for your wonderful and thought-provoking illustrations.

Isha Nagar, a huge thank you for the fine details you've added to further underscore the spirit of the book and for the delightful cover design.

My dear friend, Kinnari, and the kids, Arinjay, Vivikt, Ayan, and Rehaan, thank you so much for bearing with me while I pored over every installation at the Linguistic Diversity of India exhibition held at the Nehru Science Centre in Mumbai.

Last but not the least, truly grateful to authors, historians, journalists, linguists, professors, researchers, bloggers across the length and breadth of our country, who have written about our languages and whose stories and articles have added to the knowledge that this book contains.

There is hope for the future of our languages and my sincere thanks to every reader who will read this book and embark on a journey to preserve their mother tongues for generations to come.

Love,

Vaishali

READ MORE BY THE AUTHOR

Welcome to Chitwan National Park!

As big as 1,78,000 football fields, Nepal's first protected national park is home to over 550 species of birds; awe-inspiring animals, such as greater one-horned rhinoceroses, Bengal tigers, clouded leopards; and a confident, brave girl called Sita.

Sita dreams of being a nature guide like her baba. With a spring in her step and a group of eager tourists, she unravels the secrets of the forest. But when she wanders astray and comes face to face with a mamma rhino, will this eight-year-old be able to listen to the stillness of the jungle?

Join this young Nepali as she takes you on a tour of the magnificent UNESCO World Heritage Site.